NEW YORK CITY MONUMENTS *of* BLACK AMERICANS

A History and Guide

DAVID FELSEN

Foreword by Sonia Sanchez

THE History PRESS

Published by The History Press
An imprint of Arcadia Publishing
Charleston, SC
www.historypress.com

Frontispiece maps created by Jim McMahon; graphic design by Keirsten Geise.

First published 2025

Manufactured in the United States

ISBN 9781467159050

Library of Congress Control Number: 2025934494

Art must discover and reveal the beauty which prejudice and caricature have obscured and over-laid.

—*Alain Locke,* The New Negro *(1925)*

NEW JERSEY
NEW YORK
INWOOD
Bronx Community College
THE BRONX
Hudson River
Henry Hudson Pkwy.
Sedgwick Ave.
Riverside Dr.
Harlem River Dr.
W 155th St.
Broadway
Amsterdam Ave.
Frederick Douglass Blvd.
Adam Clayton Powell Jr. Blvd.
Grand Concourse
Morningside Park
HARLEM
Dr. Martin Luther King Jr. Blvd.
Harlem River
W 110th St.
Randalls and Wards Islands
Rikers Island
Central Park West
Central Park
5th Ave.
Park Ave.
FDR Dr.
W 42nd St.
E 59th St.
MIDTOWN MANHATTAN
MANHATTAN
East River
W 14nd St.
Broadway
LOWER MANHATTAN
FINANCIAL DISTRICT
FDR Dr.
0
1 MI
N
S
E
W
NYC Black Statues
4 Africa, The Four Continents, 1907
5 Carl Schurz, 1913
8 Cotton, Industries of the British Empire, 1933
9 Woman, the Mother and Housekeeper & Man, the Provider, 1938
11 Colonel William Hayward, 1945
12 Booker T. Washington, 1946
13 Lincoln and Child, 1949
14 Coast Guard Memorial, 1955
15 Young George Washington Carver, 1955
16 Martin Luther King, Jr., 1970
17 George Washington Carver, 1977
18 Jackie Robinson, 1981
22 Duke Ellington, 1997
24 Invisible Man, Ralph Ellison, 2003
25 Adam Clayton Powell, Jr., 2005
27 Swing Low, Harriet Tubman, 2008
28 Frederick Douglass, 2011
30 Sojourner Truth, Women's Rights Pioneers, 2020

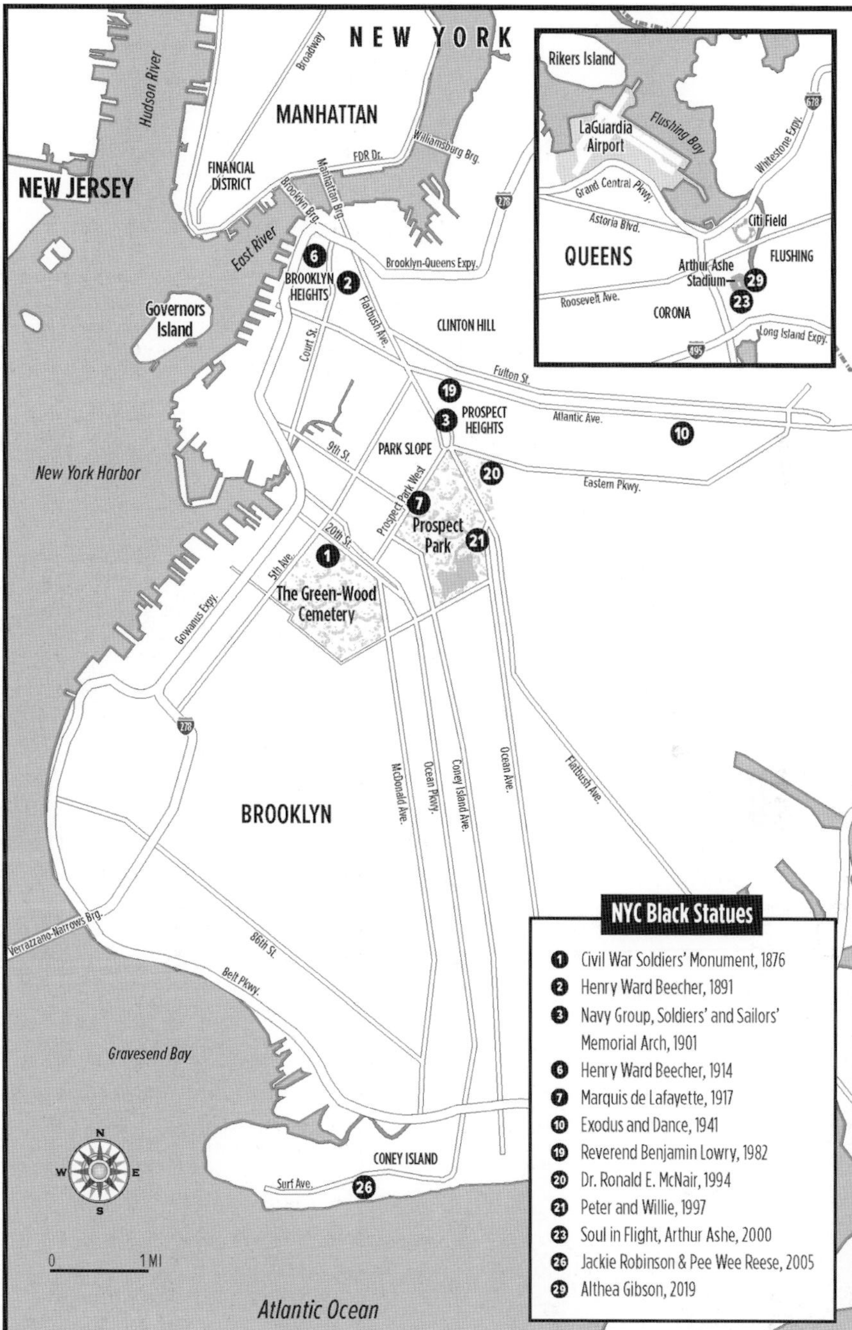
NEW YORK
MANHATTAN
NEW JERSEY
FINANCIAL DISTRICT
Hudson River
East River
Broadway
FDR Dr.
Williamsburg Brg.
Manhattan Brg.
Brooklyn Brg.
Brooklyn-Queens Expy.
BROOKLYN HEIGHTS
Governors Island
CLINTON HILL
Court St.
Flatbush Ave.
Fulton St.
Atlantic Ave.
PROSPECT HEIGHTS
PARK SLOPE
9th St.
Prospect Park West
Eastern Pkwy.
New York Harbor
Prospect Park
20th St.
5th Ave.
The Green-Wood Cemetery
Gowanus Expy.
BROOKLYN
McDonald Ave.
Ocean Pkwy.
Coney Island Ave.
Ocean Ave.
Flatbush Ave.
Verrazzano-Narrows Brg.
86th St.
Belt Pkwy.
Gravesend Bay
CONEY ISLAND
Surf Ave.
Atlantic Ocean
0 1 MI
N
S
E
W
Rikers Island
LaGuardia Airport
Flushing Bay
Grand Central Pkwy.
Whitestone Expy.
Astoria Blvd.
Citi Field
QUEENS
FLUSHING
Arthur Ashe Stadium
Roosevelt Ave.
CORONA
Long Island Expy.
NYC Black Statues
1 Civil War Soldiers' Monument, 1876
2 Henry Ward Beecher, 1891
3 Navy Group, Soldiers' and Sailors' Memorial Arch, 1901
6 Henry Ward Beecher, 1914
7 Marquis de Lafayette, 1917
10 Exodus and Dance, 1941
19 Reverend Benjamin Lowry, 1982
20 Dr. Ronald E. McNair, 1994
21 Peter and Willie, 1997
23 Soul in Flight, Arthur Ashe, 2000
26 Jackie Robinson & Pee Wee Reese, 2005
29 Althea Gibson, 2019

CONTENTS

Foreword

SISTER ELIZABETH CATLETT

Author's note: Sonia Sanchez is a beautiful human being, an award-winning poet and a national treasure. She is also the mother of my closest childhood friends, Mungu and Morani. When I asked Mrs. Sanchez to write the foreword to this book, she shared the following remembrance and haiku about the artist Elizabeth Catlett, whose Invisible Man: A Memorial to Ralph Ellison *is among the monuments featured in these pages.*

I don't remember the first time I met Elizabeth Catlett. I don't remember what I was doing. There was no remembered witness to my doings, but it seems as if I had known her forever. She who has moved through mornings and midnites, through death and dawns to document our bones. Blood. Herstory.

I remember the last time I saw her in New York City. She arrived breathing a quiet grace. She stretched out her hands to us all, those hands neither mother nor daughter. Father nor son. But family. Full of information. Beauty. Scriptures. Carousels. Courage. A courage that makes us glimpse ourselves celebrating ourselves, our lives instead of our massacres. So I am here to honor, celebrate a woman who honored us all with her hands. Eyes. Heart. Life. Who was brilliant enough to give us Black men and women who were Blacker than our unhurried laughter. How to celebrate a woman whose hands are a blue sash of rain raining convocation of flesh? How to make you remember her voice downpouring yellow butterflies? How to remember those fastidious hands, those hands that got up in the nite and followed voices lying in wake in the dark for paintings being sung from chandeliers?

I guess I will just praise her worth, her voice, her hands, hand-painting us together on an afternoon when the spaces between us smile; I guess I will lift up my eyes to this extraordinary Woman/Artist/Mother/Wife tasting the sea with her blood. I guess I will just say: listen. Listen. Listen. Hear her incredible crease of laughter. Listen. Listen. Listen to the exact wings exacting breath from the clouds. Listen. Listen. Listen to this woman of prayer and canons. Listen to this woman of trees and oceans. Listen to her songs that ran from her hands to her heart. Listen as we lean into her canvas, scoop lightning from her pores as she continues her woman clear art.

Sonia Sanchez
Winter 2024

6 Haiku (for Elizabeth Catlett in Cuernavaca)

1.
La Señora
making us remember
flesh and wind

2.
O how you
help us catch
each other's breath

3.
a woman's
arms climbing with
colored dreams

4.
Elizabeth
slides into the pool
hands kissing the water

5.
i pick
up your breath and
remember me

6.
your hands
humming hurricanes
of beauty.

ACKNOWLEDGEMENTS

There are so many people to thank! I would like to start with my high school history teacher and baseball coach, Harry Gratwick, whose books on *The Forts of Maine* and *Mainers in the Civil War* are a must for fans of the Pine Tree State. Mr. Gratwick not only inspired and encouraged me to write this book, but he also generously shared his contacts with me at The History Press. Many thanks to the great American historian and professor emeritus at Haverford College Roger Lane. Roger made history fun, and he generously gave me feedback on elements of this book even though I graduated in 1992! I'm grateful to the Gilder Lehrman Institute of American History master's program, especially Professor Andrew Robertson's Historiography and Historical Methods class, which nudged me toward my unhealthy obsession with monuments and gave me the tools I needed to complete this work.

I have many people and institutions to thank for their research assistance on this project. Julianna Monjeau, the archivist at New York City's Public Design Commission, shared many illuminating documents and images in a timely and friendly fashion. Cynthia Tobar at the Bronx Community College Hall of Fame for Great Americans Archive found several engrossing boxes of files on its Booker T. Washington and George Washington Carver busts for me to comb through. Green-Wood Cemetery historian Jeff Richman kindly set me straight about Black Union soldiers on the cemetery's grounds. Additional thanks to the Schomburg Center for Research in Black Culture, the Prospect Park Alliance Archive, the New York City Municipal Archives and the La Guardia Wagner Archive NYCHA Collection. The digital collections of the following archives were invaluable sources of most of the archival images in this book: the New York Public Library, the Brooklyn Public Library, the Library of Congress and the National Archives.

In addition to having the most amazing job in the city (director of art and antiquities for the New York City Parks Department) and the coolest office address in the city (Northwest Turret, Arsenal, Central Park), Jonathan Kuhn has an encyclopedic knowledge of the Parks Department collection, which he generously shared with me on the phone and in person. I am forever grateful for his support with this project and look forward to the book that he absolutely must write about his nearly forty-year career in the wild and woolly world of the Parks Department.

Much of the way I began to think about the Black presence in American monuments was inspired by Kirk Savage's book *Standing Soldiers, Kneeling Slaves: Race, War and Monument in Nineteenth-Century America.* Savage does a remarkable job of showing how enslaved Black Americans were portrayed in sculptural monuments before, during and after the Civil War. I cannot recommend this book highly enough. Michele Bogart's books *Public Sculpture and the Civic Ideal in New York City, 1890–1930* and *Sculpture in Gotham Art and Urban Renewal in New York City* are indispensable. I also want to thank her for a very encouraging phone call early in this process. Dianne Durante's *Outdoor Monuments of Manhattan* also served as a model for how to think about sculpture and how to write a guidebook. Diane was even kind enough to Zoom in for a memorable talk with my high school history students a few years ago as we emerged from the COVID-19 pandemic. Harlem historian John Reddick generously met with me about the role of community engagement in public memorials. Do not miss his upcoming book about Black and Jewish music culture and Tin Pan Alley.

I want to thank my amazing colleagues at Avenues the World School, in the "Bunker" and beyond, for being a reliable source of joy, knowledge and encouragement. My US history students have occasionally served as unsuspecting guinea pigs for some of the passages in this guide, and I appreciate their curiosity, feedback and kind support. Yes, Kieran, that means you.

Thank you to the lovely and talented Dave Jacobs—yes, that Dave Jacobs. Dave generously gave of his time for this project, and his photos, which grace this book, add a touch of class to the whole affair. What a mensch! If you find yourself in Carroll Gardens, stop by his Court Street gallery Plant486 for some cheap wine and witty badinage.

I am grateful to Sonia Sanchez for her twins, Mongu and Morani, my best childhood friends; for welcoming me into her home; for introducing me to health food; for her poetry; for her spirit; and for those treasured conversations about her astounding life. Sonia is a bona fide national treasure, and I am so honored that she agreed to write the foreword.

Thank you to my brother, sisters, niece and nephew, cousins, aunts and uncles, for politely asking how the book was going and patiently listening to my answers. To Andrea Yayura Clark, whose compelling book *On the Night of a Thousand Stars* was an inspiration. To my mother, Kitty, for knowing everything there is to know about everything and teaching me to love history. To my father, David Sr., whose boundless support in all areas is beyond measure, and whose love of Jackie Robinson, teaching and justice surely has something to do with this book. To my son, Clyde, who makes me so proud and who is becoming a sharp and probing historian in his own right. To Nala and Biggie for their warmth. Love and appreciation to all of you.

And thank you to my amazing wife, Sally Herships, whom I simply could not have done this without. Over the past two years, Sally generously shared her public radio reporter storytelling talent. She edited every word of this book, asked lots of questions (the way she does) and just made it better. Dearest Sally, thank you so much. I love you!

David Felsen Jr.

INTRODUCTION

New York City got its first monument of a real Black American in 1946 when the Hall of Fame for Great Americans in the Bronx dedicated a bronze bust to Booker T. Washington. Behind every first is a story of triumph over adversity and exclusion. This is the history of how New York City got its monuments to Black Americans.

In 2015, nine African Americans were murdered by a white supremacist at the Mother Emanuel AME Church in Charleston, South Carolina. In the wake of their deaths, people began to call for the removal of Confederate memorials, and cities and towns throughout the South complied. The removal movement gained further momentum following the Unite the Right rally in Charlottesville in 2017 and George Floyd's murder in Minneapolis in 2020. By 2021, hundreds of Confederate statues had been removed, including Richmond's Robert E. Lee Monument, which was dedicated in 1890.

At this time, when the media and academics were paying so much attention to problematic Confederate monuments and the white men on them, it seemed too little attention was being paid to the representation of Black people in monuments. As a history teacher living in New York City, I began to wonder how many monuments of Black Americans there were in the city. Who was the first Black American honored, and when did it happen? Who were the artists, activists and civic leaders behind these monuments? Why did they get made? And what could they teach us about New York history, Black history, art history and American history?

This guide is an attempt to answer these questions, but I also wrote it because I believe that monuments matter. They matter in New York City and beyond as public history, sites of memory that ask us to consider the past, its people and their continuing legacy. They matter because they reflect the values of the city and how they have changed over time. They matter as public art, as inspiring displays of vision and skill by some of the greatest sculptors of the past century and a half. They matter because art matters. And they matter in particular for Black Americans because the way they are portrayed in statues, as in literature, Hollywood and advertising, has a complex and loaded past, a past that influences how others see them and how they see themselves.

Sculpture itself has a history of being used for racist ends. In the United States during the nineteenth century, bleached Greek and Roman statues of gods and goddesses were held up as evidence of the superiority of European civilization and white supremacy. Likewise, Confederate monuments reinforced the idea of white rule in a segregated nation for over a century. At the same time, for much of our history, the symbolic representation in statues of African Americans by white sculptors has tended to reinforce the racial hierarchy and negative stereotypes.

The first appearance of a Black person in a New York City monument came in Brooklyn's Green-Wood Cemetery as the United States was experiencing its first memorial boom in the wake of the Civil War. In a bronze panel at the base of the Civil War Soldiers' Monument (1876), a nameless, shoeless former slave helps a Union widow to find her husband's grave in the South. The Black man in this statue is there only to help the whites. Similarly, during the City Beautiful movement of the late nineteenth and early twentieth century, when New York added heroic statues of white men like Washington and Columbus, if Black Americans appeared in statues at all, they played supporting roles in the lives of whites. The cowering slave girls in Gutzon Borglum's Henry Ward Beecher Memorial (1914) at Plymouth Church were rescued by a great white savior. A Black groom holding a horse serves a great white man in Daniel Chester French's Marquis de Lafayette Memorial (1917) in Prospect Park. If Black figures were alone, they were fulfilling a negative stereotype, like French's sleeping sculpture of Africa at the Alexander Hamilton U.S. Custom House in 1907.

It wasn't until 1938 that Black New Yorkers began to have a say about monuments in their community, like *Man, the Provider* and *Woman, the Mother and Housekeeper* at the Harlem River Houses and *Exodus and Dance* at Brooklyn's Kingsborough Houses. This was made possible in part by the emergence of Richmond Barthé, a Black sculptor who assisted on the former and was completely responsible for the latter, and the rise in the city's Black population brought on by the Great Migration. And yet, just a few years later, in 1943, the Museum of Natural History dedicated a statue of a mounted Teddy Roosevelt with a half-naked Black man and a Native American flanking him on foot. In 2022, following public complaints that the monument was a symbol of racism and colonialism, it was removed.

After a bust by Barthé of Booker T. Washington broke the monument color barrier in 1946, it was followed, haltingly, by George Washington Carver at the Carver Houses in 1955 and Martin Luther King Jr. at the Esplanade Gardens apartment building in Harlem in 1970. Only in the 1990s, as public funding for monuments increased and Black political influence grew, did dedications of monuments honoring Black American men driven by Black New Yorkers become more regular events, with the likes of astronaut Ronald McNair, writer Ralph Ellison and civil rights leader Adam Clayton Powell Jr. joining the pantheon. More often than not, the sculptors behind these statues, Ogundipe Fayomi, Elizabeth Catlett and Branly Cadet, were also Black.

To the city's eternal shame, there were no monuments of Black American women until the Swing Low: Harriet Tubman Memorial in Harlem in 2008 by the Black artist Alison Saar. Tubman was followed by Althea Gibson in 2019 and Sojourner Truth in 2020, but the lack of Black female representation is telling. It is also consistent. As of this writing, there are just seven statues of real women of any race in the city. Similarly, there are no monuments of real Native Americans, Chinese Americans or Latino Americans. A monument to the first Black woman elected to the House of Representatives, Brooklyn's Shirley Chisolm, is planned for Prospect Park in 2025.

METHODOLOGY

There are many plaques, markers, abstract sculptures and even large-scale monuments, like the African Burial Ground, honoring Black Americans in the city. However, because this guide is concerned with public images of Black Americans, I chose to focus only on publicly accessible statues and bas-reliefs: works in which faces and bodies are clearly depicted. By my unofficial count, there are thirty monuments in the city that fit this description.

To arrive at this number, I relied on a few sources. I turned first to the City Parks Art and Antiquities Division's online catalogue. Out of over

800 public monuments in its public collection, 250 are sculptures, and of those, 125 honor historical figures. Of the monuments in this guide, 17 come from this remarkable collection. Others I found in the Municipal Art Society's Manhattan sculpture guide and Cal Fury's *Out of Fire and Valor: The War Memorials of New York*. Online sources like Monument Lab's National Monument Audit and the Smithsonian Art Inventories Catalog were also helpful. I even found one through sheer dumb luck. While leading a class of high school students around Rockefeller Center, I looked up to see a small gold figure of a Black woman representing "Cotton" above the main entrance to the British Empire Building, which I had no idea existed. She is now in the book.

There are a few statues that came close but did not qualify. I left out a portrait statue of Frederick Douglass on the steps of the New York Historical Society because the public played no role in putting it there. There's a bust of Martin Luther King Jr. at Brooklyn College that didn't make it because it's not easily accessed by the public. That said, I did include a World War I memorial with the Harlem Hellfighters at the Harlem Armory that is generally not accessible to the public because I thought the story behind it was too important to leave out. Finally, I would not be at all surprised if I somehow managed to overlook a monument that belongs in this guide. For this, and any other errors or omissions, I apologize in advance.

How to Use This Guide

This guide is a series of thirty essays chronologically organized to tell the story of how Black Americans have been represented in New York City's monuments and how that representation has changed over time. You are, of course, welcome to enjoy the stories behind the monuments and all the wonderful images at your leisure wherever you like to read, but nothing beats going to see a monument in person. These are three-dimensional objects in space that can only be fully appreciated live.

I've had the pleasure of seeing all the monuments in the guide, and each visit was its own adventure, either to a part of the city where I'd never been or to a familiar neighborhood that the monument helped me see in a new light. I strongly urge you to use the map and make a plan to visit any of these monuments on foot or by bike (my favorite), bus, subway or car in Brooklyn, Manhattan, the Bronx and Queens.

Chapter 1

CIVIL WAR SOLDIERS' MONUMENT

Undated stereograph of the Civil War Soldiers' Monument. *New York Public Library.*

SCULPTOR: Henry Jackson Ellicott (1847–1901)
DEDICATED: May 29, 1876
LOCATION: Battle Hill, Green-Wood Cemetery, Brooklyn
ARCHITECT: Unknown
MATERIALS: Bronze
SIZE: H: 35'
DONOR: New York City Common Council

Inscription:

> *ERECTED ANNO DOMINI 1869. THE CITY OF NEW-YORK DEDICATES THIS MONUMENT TO ITS HEROIC DEAD. THE CITY OF NEW-YORK ENLISTED 148,000 CITIZENS IN AID OF THE WAR FOR THE PRESERVATION OF THE UNION AND THE CONSTITUTION. EVER REMEMBER HOW MUCH THE NATIONAL PROSPERITY IS DUE TO THE BRAVE EXERTIONS OF THE SOLDIERS WHO DIED IN SERVICE OF THEIR COUNTRY.*

One has to look closely to find the Black man in Green-Wood Cemetery's Civil War Soldiers' Monument, but push your way through the plantings to the bottom of a thirty-five foot granite Corinthian column and you'll see him there on a bronze plaque. Shoeless, he stands with a hat in his left hand while reaching out with his right to comfort a kneeling, weeping white woman and her child by a soldier's grave. He has no name, but he is likely the first Black person depicted in a New York City monument.

Surrounded by the graves of soldiers who died in the war as well as veterans, the monument sits on Battle Hill, a high point with a remarkable view of New York Harbor and lower Manhattan. At its base stand four life-size bronze statues by Henry Jackson Ellicott representing Union infantry, cavalry, artillery and engineers. The Black man is in one of four bas-relief bronze plaques on the column, also by Ellicott, depicting scenes from the life and death of a Union soldier. The man appears to be guiding a Union widow and her son to her husband's grave. The palmetto trees in the background suggest the scene is taking place in the South. The Black man, like all the white figures in this memorial, is a symbolic character, not an actual historical person. He is also not a central character in the drama unfolding on the bas-relief; he is part of the supporting cast. Moreover, while there were many monuments to historical white men in New York at that time, there would be none of historical Black men until the Booker T. Washington statue at the Hall of Fame for Great Americans in the Bronx in 1946.

On May 28, 1876, Memorial Day, the centennial of the American Revolution, the monument was dedicated before a crowd of thousands. An inscription on the monument reads, "The City of New York enlisted 148,000 citizens in aid of the war for the preservation of the Union and the Constitution." According to the *Brooklyn Eagle*, the Democrat boss Judge John Delmar, in his remarks, reminded the crowd that they were gathered to honor the men who died "while fighting bravely to preserve

A former slave (*right*) shows a Union widow and child to her husband's grave in this Civil War Soldiers' Monument bronze bas relief panel. *David Jacobs.*

the government of our fathers." Similarly, the "orator of the day," Civil War veteran Major Willard Bullard, praised New Yorkers from all walks of life who had volunteered to fight and "died for their country in the war for the Union."[1] Oddly, there was no mention of the four thousand African Americans from New York State who also fought for the Union. Even today, among the five thousand graves of Union soldiers in Green-Wood, just four have been identified as belonging to Black Union soldiers, one of whom was Quartermaster Sergeant John Munroe, who served in the Thirty-Fifth New York Infantry Regiment.[2] The figure of the Black man on the bronze plaque is the only reminder in the cemetery of one of the Union's central goals in the war: the emancipation of enslaved people.

It should come as no surprise that emancipation and the role of Black soldiers were ignored in the *Soldiers' Monument*. The monument was proposed and funded by New York City's Common Council, today's City Council, and it reflected the council members' values and those of their constituents. At the time of the dedication, African Americans made up less than 2 percent of New York City's and Brooklyn's populations, and their political influence was limited. Also, support in the North for Reconstruction was waning, leading to its premature end in 1877 with the withdrawal of federal troops from the South. At this time, the views of the Tammany Hall Democrats in New York, a city that had strong political and commercial ties to the South, were clear. Just six years earlier, a Tammany Hall candidate ran for state office on the slogan "No suffrage nor negro equality! White man's government for white men! White men shall rule America!"[3] It is at least consistent that these same Democrats who opposed emancipation in the Thirteenth Amendment, Black equality in the Fourteenth Amendment and the right of Black men to vote in the Fifteenth Amendment would be eager to focus on the heroism of white soldiers fighting to preserve the Union, not the contributions of Black soldiers or the emancipation of slaves.

Just a month after the dedication of the *Soldiers' Monument* in Green-Wood, another Civil War monument was dedicated in Holyoke, Massachusetts. This *Soldiers' Monument* was also, as it happened, the work of Ellicott and included the same bas-relief plaques as the Brooklyn monument. But while the visual message was essentially the same, the dedications were different in at least one significant respect. The featured speaker, Charles Wesley Slack, was a radical Republican, a known abolitionist and a strong supporter of Reconstruction. According to the *Springfield Republican*, after praising the monument and the gallantry of the veterans, Slack went on to say, "The arms of the union did not begin to triumph until suffrage was conferred on all citizens."[4] In Holyoke, Slack, unlike his counterparts at the Brooklyn dedication, wanted his audience to remember that the Civil War, in addition to being a fight to preserve the Union, was a stage in the liberation of enslaved African Americans that included the passage of the Fifteenth Amendment, giving Black men the right to vote after the war. In Republican Holyoke, Slack placed the ongoing struggle for Black rights at the center of his speech. In Democratic Brooklyn, it was ignored.

Chapter 2

HENRY WARD BEECHER MONUMENT

Henry Ward Beecher Monument in downtown Brooklyn between 1900 and 1906. *Library of Congress.*

SCULPTOR: John Quincy Adams Ward (1830–1910)
DEDICATED: June 24, 1891
LOCATION: Cadman Plaza on Johnson Street, Brooklyn
ARCHITECT: Richard Morris Hunt (1827–1895)
MATERIALS: Bronze and barre granite
SIZE: Beecher figure H: 7'6"; pedestal H × W × D: 7' × 10' × 8'5"
DONOR: Public subscription

Inscription:

> *HENRY WARD BEECHER, 1813–1887. THE GRATEFUL GIFT OF MULTITUDES OF ALL CLASSES CREEDS AND CONDITIONS AT HOME AND ABROAD TO HONOR THE GREAT APOSTLE OF THE BROTHERHOOD OF MAN.*

At the base of the Henry Ward Beecher Monument, a barefoot Black girl looks up to Beecher while laying palm fronds at his feet. On the opposite side of the statue, a small white boy and girl, also barefoot, have just placed a garland on the pediment. The white children and the Black girl are symbolic figures. The white children are meant to remind the public of Beecher's great love for youth. The Black girl most likely represents Rose Ward, a child that Beecher, an ardent abolitionist, set free from his pulpit at Plymouth Church in a "reverse slave auction." Hers is arguably the first bronze statue of Black person in a public monument in New York City. The only other Black presence at this point seems to be a hard-to-spot Black man on a plaque in Green-Wood Cemetery's Civil War Soldiers' Monument. Consistent with the depiction of African Americans in this period, her role is to support the narrative of a great white man's life.

Henry Ward Beecher was an internationally recognized abolitionist, a women's rights advocate and a charismatic pastor of the Plymouth Congregational Church in Brooklyn Heights. His older sister, Harriet Beecher Stowe, wrote the best-selling book of the nineteenth century after the Bible, *Uncle Tom's Cabin*. Beecher demonstrated his commitment to abolition by not only preaching against the evils of slavery but also raising money to buy Sharps rifles for settlers fighting to keep Kansas from becoming a slave state. During a meeting promoting emigration to Kansas, Beecher claimed "there was more power in one of these instruments, so far as the slaveholders of Kansas were concerned, as there was in one hundred bibles."[5] The rifles were shipped in crates labeled "Books and Bibles" to Kansas, where they became known as Beecher's Bibles. In 1861, Kansas entered the Union as a free state.

The monument to Beecher stands in Brooklyn's Cadman Plaza, just a short walk from Plymouth Church, where he made his fame.[6] The statue is the work of John Quincy Adams Ward (1830–1910). Known as the Dean of American Sculptors, Ward was a master at rendering portrait statues in bronze in the heroic realist style typical of the Gilded Age. Ward (no relation to Beecher) won the commission for the statue in part because he personally

Left: Henry Ward Beecher, circa 1875. *Beinecke Rare Book and Manuscript Library.*

Right: Sculptor John Quincy Adams Ward. *Archives of American Art.*

took a death mask of the preacher after his passing, thinking Beecher might be a good subject for a statue. The sculptor also used photographs of Beecher and a coat he had worn in his later years as references to show his true character. The effect gives one the sense of being in the presence of the man himself.

When Beecher died in 1887, a monument executive committee of prominent Brooklyn citizens formed, including Ripley Ropes, director of the Brooklyn Trust Company bank, and John Hunter, director of the Brooklyn Institute of the Arts, now the Brooklyn Museum. Significantly, one member of the committee, the Reverend William Thomas Dixon (1833–1909), was a Black American. Dixon was minister to a large congregation at Brooklyn's Concord Baptist Church at 165 Duffield Street, a short walk from the monument itself. The church, founded by abolitionists in 1847, was a stop on the Underground Railroad before the Civil War. Following Beecher's death, Dixon and his fellow Black clergymen released a statement of sympathy: "In Henry Ward Beecher our race has lost a staunch friend and champion, one who was always found ready to plead the cause of the slave and to aid in the work of his education."[7]

W. T. DIXON.

Reverend W.T. Dixon, 1887. *New York Public Library.*

Both an educator and a preacher, Dixon was beloved in his church, where he served for nearly fifty years, from 1863 to 1909. According to an early history of Black Americans, "Many faces brighten and hearts ring with joy when his name is called."[8] Dixon was a busy man. In a *Standard Union* piece on a celebration of his twenty-five years in the pulpit, it was estimated that during his tenure he had "baptized 637 people, preached 3,422 sermons, solemnized 360 marriages, served at 1,275 funerals, made 5,400 calls on the sick and made a total of 37,760 visits."[9] In 1897, the fiftieth anniversary of the church, Dixon reported that the congregation had 813 members, making it one of Brooklyn's largest churches. At a time when schools and churches were mostly segregated, Black churches like Dixon's were critical centers for Brooklyn's free Black communities. To this day, Concord Baptist Church serves the people of Brooklyn from its 833 Marcy Avenue location in Bedford Stuyvesant.

Dixon's selection to the committee was unusual enough to be singled out for comment in local papers, including the *New York Times*, which referred to him as a "colored divine."[10] Dixon was seated among the dignitaries on June 24, 1891, when the Beecher statue was unveiled before an estimated fifteen thousand people packed into Brooklyn's City Hall park and below the Fulton elevated train. Over seventy years later, as part of a renovation of the area, the city moved the statue to Columbus Park in Cadman Plaza. The money to build the statue came through a public subscription, a common means of raising money for public statues at the time. Starting in 1887, the Beecher monument fund raised nearly $35,000 (over $1 million today) from small and large donations. In a sign of the growing civic involvement and influence of the Black community in Brooklyn, some of those contributions came from William T. Dixon and his congregation.

Chapter 3

NAVY GROUP, SOLDIERS' AND SAILORS' MEMORIAL ARCH

Black sailor (*kneeling*) in the Navy Group on the Soldiers' and Sailors' Memorial Arch, 1904. *Library of Congress.*

SCULPTOR: Frederick William MacMonnies (1863–1937)
DEDICATED: 1901
LOCATION: Soldiers' and Sailors' Memorial Arch, Grand Army Plaza, Brooklyn
ARCHITECT: Stanford White (1853–1906)
MATERIALS: Bronze
DONOR: Veterans of the Grand Army and the New York State Legislature

Inscription:

TO THE DEFENDERS OF THE UNION 1861–1865

New York City's only public statue of a Black Civil War sailor kneels beside a cannon on the deck of a ship, surrounded by his comrades. He is part of a boarding party. His pistol is cocked, and he scans the horizon. He is shirtless and shoeless, as is one of his white shipmates. The sailor is part of the Navy Group, a high relief bronze on the southern facade of the east pier on the Soldiers' and Sailors' Memorial Arch in Brooklyn's Grand Army Plaza. For generations, the arch has been the site of Brooklyn's Memorial Day parade; more recently, Black Lives Matter protests took place there after the murder of George Floyd. The arch stands at the intersection of Flatbush Avenue, Prospect Park West, Eastern Parkway and Vanderbilt Avenue and across the street from two worlds of wonder: Prospect Park and Brooklyn's Central Library.

Inspired by Paris's Arc de Triomphe and Rome's Titus Arch, the monument is adorned with allegorical sculpture by Brooklyn native Frederick MacMonnies. MacMonnies honed his craft at the prestigious École des Beaux-Arts in Paris. At the time of this commission, he was perhaps best known for a bronze portrait statue of the Revolutionary War hero Nathan Hale in Manhattan's City Hall Park. Atop the arch is the Triumphal Progress of Columbia, a woman in a chariot pulled by four horses, the traditional Roman symbol for victory known as a quadriga. Two bronze sculpture groups, including the Navy Group in high relief by MacMonnies, were added to the face of the monument in 1901. On the left as one faces the arch is the Army Group and to the right the Navy Group, subtitled "American Sailors Boarding a Vessel at Sea Urged on by the Genius of Patriotism." The naked Genius of Patriotism, with an American Eagle by her side, stands atop the group, while the Black sailor kneels at the bottom. Like all the sailors in the group, he is not identified.

The memorial arch, funded by the Grand Army of the Republic, a Civil War veterans association, and the New York State Legislature, was dedicated on October 21, 1892, as part of massive Columbus Day celebrations. The inscription on the arch reads, "To the defenders of the Union," and at the unveiling attended by thousands, in a pattern that echoed the dedication of the Civil War Soldiers' Monument in Green-Wood Cemetery, the speeches of Brooklyn Mayor Boody and many others identified the restoration of the Union as the only purpose for the war. Only one speaker, E.W. McCarty, the

Soldiers' and Sailors' Memorial Arch, 1904. *Library of Congress.*

white reverend of Saint Augustine's Church in Brooklyn, chose to remind the public that the soldiers and sailors fought not only to preserve the Union in the land that Columbus discovered but also to "wipe from off its handsome face the ugly stain of slavery."[11]

During the Civil War, of the more than one hundred thousand men who joined the Union navy, roughly eighteen thousand were Black. Black sailors, denied the opportunity to become officers, served as either cooks, stewards or musicians. But in combat, when the bullets started flying, they were still expected to fight, manning guns and joining boarding parties alongside their white crewmates. Many of these men fought with distinction, including Joachim Pease of the USS *Kearsarge*, who was awarded the Medal of Honor for his actions in the sinking of the CSS *Alabama* off the coast of Cherbourg, France, on June 19, 1864. According to the citation, while serving as a gun loader, "Pease exhibited marked coolness and good conduct and was highly recommended by the divisional officer for gallantry under fire." Unfortunately, Pease left the navy before he could receive the medal, and no record of his life after his service has been found.[12]

It's unclear what reaction, if any, the Black press had to the rare appearance of a Black figure in such a prominent public sculpture or to the fact that in the hierarchy of the work, as in society, he was at the bottom. The *Brooklyn Eagle*, in its review of the Navy Group, pointed out the presence of the Black sailor but offered no commentary on its significance. One man who had strong feelings about the statue and all statues that included African Americans was the Black activist and art historian Freeman Murray (1859–1950). In his 1916 book *Emancipation and the Freed in American Sculpture: A Study in Interpretation*, Murray argued that "the portrayal of Black Folk in art" in general and in sculpture in particular was especially important to African Americans in a segregated society. "We cannot be too concerned," he wrote, "as to what they [monuments] say or suggest, or what they leave unsaid." To Murray, the Black sailor on the arch was a success for "Black Folk," regardless of its position. He referred to it as "MacMonnies' Black Hero" and had high praise for that artist "who [having]...admitted a Negro to an honorable place in this valorous group, had also included in it others of the principal racial and national extractions which unitedly compose this great nation." For Murray, the Navy Group was a rare vision of racial unity, one that evoked the memory of the 1889 unveiling in Boston of the Crispus Attucks Monument for the victims of the Boston Massacre. Attucks, a man of color, was thought to be the first American killed in the Revolution. Murray summed up his review of the Navy Group by quoting from the poem "Crispus Attucks," read by the poet John Boyle O'Reilly (1844–1890) at that dedication:

> *Indian and Negro, Saxon and Celt, Teuton and Latin and Gaul—*
> *Mere surface shadow and sunshine, while the sounding unifies all*
> *One love, one hope, one duty theirs: no matter the time or ken,*
> *There never was separate heart-beat in all the races of men.*

One could accuse Murray of having an overly rosy vision of the racial harmony depicted by the statue, but considering that he was writing in 1916, when the country and the military were segregated, perhaps that's easier to understand. As he wrote, "Under the anomalous conditions prevailing in this country, any recognition of Black Folk in art works which are intended for public view, is apt to be pleasing to us."

Chapter 4

AFRICA, THE FOUR CONTINENTS

Africa, one of Daniel Chester French's *Four Continents*. *Carol M. Highsmith.*

SCULPTOR: Daniel Chester French (1850–1931)
DEDICATED: 1907
LOCATION: Alexander Hamilton U.S. Custom House, Bowling Green, New York
ARCHITECT: Cass Gilbert (1859–1934)
MATERIALS: Marble
SIZE: Pedestal: 9'; statues: 9.5' to 11"
DONOR: Commissioned by U.S. Department of the Treasury

The Black woman sits naked from the waist up. Her head nods forward, and her eyes are closed. Her right arm rests on the Great Sphinx of Giza, and her left on a lion couchant. Crouching at her back is a mysterious veiled figure. The Black woman is *Africa*—or, at least, how the sculptor Daniel Chester French chose to represent the continent in his statues of the Four Continents for the entrance to the Alexander Hamilton U.S. Custom House.

When it opened in 1907, the $4.5 million dollar customhouse was the most expensive building in New York City, save the infamously overpriced Tweed Courthouse in City Hall Park. The Beaux Arts customhouse was part of the City Beautiful movement, a public works program starting in the 1890s that sought to make urban areas beautiful and inspiring places. Other prime examples in New York include the Metropolitan Museum (1902), the New York Public Library (1911) and Grand Central Station (1913). Like all these buildings, the customhouse was intended to announce New York as one of the great cosmopolitan centers of the world. In 1905, before the passage of the Sixteenth Amendment and the advent of federal income tax, eight years later, customs duties on imported goods were the federal government's main source of income. In fact, half of the nation's annual revenue came from customs duties, and a remarkable three quarters of that came through New York City.[13]

Postcard of the Alexander Hamilton U.S. Custom House between 1904 and 1910. *New York Public Library.*

Sculptor Daniel Chester French. *New York Public Library.*

To adorn this customs building through which the wealth of the globe would flow, the architect, Cass Gilbert, wanted the best sculpture that money could buy. For the fifth-floor cornice, he commissioned heroic statues to represent a dozen pioneers in global maritime trade: Phoenicia, Greece, Rome, Genoa, Venice, Spain, Holland, Portugal, Denmark, Germany, England, France. The presence of just one non-European country (Phoenicia) in the group gives one an idea of Gilbert's limited vision of the world of trade. For the building's grand entrance, he chose Daniel Chester French to model *Four Continents: Asia, America, Europe and Africa.* French intended the allegorical marble statues to represent the primary trading partners of the United States, but they also revealed another story: the problematic racial attitudes of the time.

French, one of the greatest American sculptors of his time, is best known for his seated statue of Abraham Lincoln in the Lincoln Memorial (1922). In the early stages of the *Four Continents* project, the artist invited a reporter from the *New York Tribune* to his studio at 125 West Eleventh Street and explained the meaning of these highly symbolic works. "In the statue of Europe," French said, "I have sought to symbolize imperialism….She holds her head high as one long accustomed to command. America is progressive as shown by her aggressive attitude. The Indian crouching behind her represents the disappearance of aboriginal savagery." As for *Asia* and *Africa*, he dismissed them as "continents which contrast with those two others as stagnant pools with rushing rivers." *Asia*, he said, "sits in a stupor." *Africa* he labeled "the slumbering continent." *Africa*, the only nude among the *Four Continents*, reclines with a docile lion to her left and a weather-beaten Sphinx to her right. French drew the reporter's attention to the shrouded figure at her back, "a figure of power, alert and alive, typifying the spirit of Western Civilization which has recently begun to conquer Africa."[14] One of the aims of the City Beautiful movement was to make works of art that would teach citizens, especially newly arrived immigrants, about U.S. history and values. The lesson here is unambiguous, as far as French was concerned: the only hope for Africa was European imperialism and colonization.

French's disturbing depictions of the Native American, Asian and African characters in the *Four Continents* were consistent with pervasive white supremacist beliefs in the United States at the time. The sculptor was a great admirer of President Theodore Roosevelt, who held sincerely racist beliefs. Despite being the first president to break bread with a Black guest, Booker T. Washington, at the White House, this was the same man who would later write to his friend the author Owen Wister, "Now, as to the Negroes! I entirely agree with you that as a race and in the mass they are altogether inferior to whites."

When the *Four Continents* were installed in 1906, they were hailed as a "sculptural masterpiece" by the *New York Times*. *Century* magazine declared, "Mr. French has moved forward to a new feeling, an original method in dealing with abstract sculpture." In 1916, the Black art historian Freeman Murray, in his book on Black Americans in sculpture, raved, "These groups by French are works of exceptional distinction. 'Africa,' in particular, is a noble and admirable conception." Murray, it seems, had no issue with French depicting Africa slouching and asleep, a portrayal consistent with widespread negative stereotypes of the people and the continent in the Jim Crow era. Instead, he pointed out that after a small figure on the bronze doors of the U.S. Capitol, this statue was only the second depiction of an African American on federal property.

Still, Freeman could not ignore the central flaw of the *Africa* monument: she does not appear to be African or, more specifically, Black African. As he wrote, "'Ethiopia' is scarcely noticeably African, that is, Negroid, in features; and moreover she has long, straight hair which hangs in a smooth plait down over her bosom." Here, Freeman generously gives French the benefit of the doubt and imagines that his "unconscious race pride" caused him to give *Africa* the appearance of a white woman, thinking that Black Americans would be flattered by the "toning." French, in a letter responding to Freeman's claim, admitted as much: "I could retreat into the safe ground that I am depicting an Egyptian and so even defend the long hair…[but] it is a fact that I have, in the figure, spoken the language of European art instead of sticking closely to the African type." While Freeman saw this as a mistake, he nonetheless appeared relieved that at least French didn't make *Africa* a blatantly negative caricature of a Black woman. French, he wrote, "could have demeaned or disrespected us, as lesser men would have done and often have done." This, more than anything, speaks to how little some African Americans expected from whites at the dawn of the twentieth century.[15]

Chapter 5

CARL SCHURZ MEMORIAL

Emancipation stele in the Carl Schurz Memorial, by Karl Bitter. *David Jacobs.*

SCULPTOR: Karl Bitter (1867–1915)
DEDICATED: May 10, 1913
LOCATION: Morningside Drive at 116th Street
ARCHITECT: Henry Bacon
MATERIALS: Bronze and black diamond granite
STATUS SIZE: 8'9"
DONOR: Carl Schurz Memorial Fund

Inscription:

CARL SCHURZ, SOLDIER-STATESMAN, PHILANTHROPIST, 1829–1906

Inscription below statue:

A Defender of Liberty and a Friend of Human Rights

Carved into the face of a granite block on the memorial for esteemed German American statesman and humanitarian Carl Schurz, an unusual scene unfolds. A Black woman walks behind a Black man, her hand on his shoulder. The couple are following the helmeted goddess Athena, a symbol of freedom and democracy, who holds their chains. A seated half-nude Black woman in an Egyptian headdress looks on. Behind her, another goddess urges a Native American man to follow. The scene was the first in a public monument in New York City to celebrate emancipation. At its dedication in Morningside Heights, on a cold and windy May day in 1913, an impressive array of dignitaries gathered, including Andrew Carnegie; Count von Bernstorff, the German ambassador to the United States; and Booker T. Washington. They came because Carl Schurz was an exceptional man. A revolutionary, he fled to the United States after the failed German Revolution of 1848 and settled in Wisconsin, where he quickly mastered English and, in keeping with his democratic ideals, became a leader in the antislavery movement and the Republican Party. During the Civil War, he was appointed a major general of the Union army. Later, as secretary of the interior, he worked to improve the condition of Native Americans.

Schurz earned a sterling human rights reputation among African Americans for his revealing postwar *Report on the Condition of the South*. Released in December 1865, it detailed the abuses against freedmen by a resentful white population bent on terrorizing former slaves, whom they deemed incapable of working outside the institution of slavery, immune to education and unworthy of the vote. Schurz's work inspired Congress to keep federal troops in the former Confederacy to protect freedmen and foster Reconstruction. Speaking at Schurz's memorial service in 1906, Booker T. Washington said, "Because he lived, my race is the richer, more confident and encouraged."[16]

The Schurz memorial unveiling was both a celebration of an immigrant success story and an indicator of the economic, political and social

Senator Carl Schurz of Missouri, between 1869 and 1875. *Library of Congress.*

influence of the German community in New York—a kind of influence that was still decades away for African Americans. On Schurz's death, the memorial committee raised $93,000 in donations (nearly $3 million today) and chose the Austrian-born sculptor Karl Bitter to design the monument. Bitter's heroic bronze portrait statue of Schurz portrays him as every inch a late nineteenth-century statesman, complete with greatcoat and fedora. The inscription on the pediment reads, "A Defender of Liberty and a Friend of Human Rights."

Bitter's granite emancipation scene is done in the Archaic style, reminiscent of the funerary *stelae* of classical Greece. In its coverage of the dedication, the *New York Times* described the relief as "allegorical figures representing the principal activities of Mr. Schurz." There was no mention of Schurz the abolitionist or early advocate for Reconstruction, only that he agreed with President Lincoln that "the country could not exist with half freedom and half slavery."[17] A closer look at the emancipation scene reveals the characters representing Greek and Western civilization to be fully clothed, while the Native American and "African" people are only half-clothed. This is, sadly, consistent with the rendering of most non-whites in public sculpture at that time.

Equally problematic was Schurz's reputation as a staunch defender of Black rights. While this reputation was at first deserved, he would go on to undermine it. Elected to the United States Senate in 1868, he soon lost confidence in the Black Republican Party in the South and changed his position on Reconstruction. "Schurz," Eric Foner wrote in his history of Reconstruction, "advocated political amnesty [for former Confederates], an end to federal intervention, and a return to 'local self-government' by men of 'property and enterprise.'"[18] This meant government by white Southerners, whom Schurz naively believed would protect the rights of Blacks. Instead, it would mean a premature end to Reconstruction and the reestablishment of a white supremacy regime that remained in place until the civil rights era—and that some argue is still in place. In his critical history of Reconstruction, W.E.B. Du Bois characterized Schurz as "fair to indifferent to the Negro"—not exactly a ringing endorsement for a "defender of liberty."[19]

Chapter 6

HENRY WARD BEECHER MEMORIAL

Henry Ward Beecher Memorial, Gutzon Borglum, 1914. *David Jacobs.*

SCULPTOR: Gutzon Borglum (1867–1941)
DEDICATED: October 18, 1914
LOCATION: Plymouth Church, Brooklyn
MATERIALS: Bronze and granite
SIZE: Pedestal H: 6'3"; Beecher statue H: 8', sisters statues H: 4'5'
DONOR: Plymouth Church parishioners

Inscription:

HENRY WARD BEECHER, 1813–1887

In the years before the Civil War, Plymouth Church in Brooklyn Heights was famous throughout the nation as a hub for abolitionist activity. Frederick Douglass, William Lloyd Garrison and Sojourner Truth spoke there. Abraham Lincoln worshipped there on February 26, 1860, when he was a candidate for president, and his pew (no. 89) is still marked. The great force behind Plymouth's success was its pastor, Henry Ward Beecher, who founded the church in the Congregationalist tradition in 1849. Beecher's fiery sermons against slavery filled the Orange Street sanctuary to its 2,800-seat capacity. He famously held mock slave auctions where attendees bought the freedom of enslaved people, and there is ample evidence that he allowed the church to be used as a stop on the Underground Railroad. Only a widely publicized alleged affair with a parishioner, Elizabeth Tilton, and the subsequent adultery trial would tarnish Beecher's image. Nonetheless, shortly after his death in 1883, a group of prominent Brooklyn citizens raised money through public subscription and honored Beecher with a statue by John Quincy Adams Ward in front of Borough Hall (for more on this and Beecher's remarkable career, see page 25). Apparently, one monument honoring "the great apostle of the brotherhood of man" was not enough.

Brooklyn's second statue of Beecher came as part of an expansion of Plymouth Church overseen by church pastor Reverend Dr. Newell Dwight Hillis and funded by parishioners like coffee and sugar merchant John Arbuckle and his heirs. Determined to honor Beecher on the centennial of his birth in 1913, Hillis drove an ambitious plan, which included the construction of the Beecher Memorial Institute, a "social institute" for the continuing education of young men and women in Brooklyn Heights. The four-story building, designed by Woodruff Leeming, included classrooms, a gymnasium, an art gallery and offices for social workers.[20] The plan included an arcade with a gallery connecting the institute to the church. Beecher Garden, a pleasant green at the center of the campus, was originally intended to (but never did) hold the remains of Beecher and his wife, Eunice. Those can be found in Green-Wood Cemetery. Due to construction delays, the statue honoring Beecher, along with a relief of Abraham Lincoln, was dedicated in Beecher Garden a year after the centennial of his birth, on October 18, 1914. Thousands gathered to witness the unveiling by the pastor's two "tiny great-granddaughters." In

Sculptor Gutzon Borglum, circa 1910. *Library of Congress.*

his speech, Reverend Hillis paid tribute to Beecher, saying he "saw the wrongs of slavery clearly, felt them passionately, and acted with every drop of blood in his body."[21]

The *Standard Union* praised the bronze statue by emerging sculptor Gutzon Borglum as a "beautiful piece of work" and pointed out that while Brooklyn had honored Washington, Lincoln and Grant in bronze, Beecher alone merited two statues.[22] Ironically, Borglum's next big commission was the giant Confederate Memorial at Stone Mountain, Georgia, followed by Mount Rushmore. In a story on the memorial, two years before its dedication, the *Brooklyn Daily Eagle* described Borglum's work as depicting Beecher as he appeared in the pulpit when he auctioned off the freedom of the Edmonson sisters, who were huddled at the base of the statue. According to the *Eagle*, "One of them watches like a hunted animal, the face of the great preacher, the other nestles into her embrace."[23] Oddly, the *Eagle*'s coverage of the dedication referred to them just as "two young slave girls" and didn't identify them by name or tell their remarkable story.

Emily and Mary Edmonson were born into slavery in Montgomery County, Maryland, in the 1830s. Their mother, Amelia, was enslaved, and their father, Paul, was a free Black man. In their teens, the girls were hired out to work in private homes in Washington, D.C. But on the night of April 15, 1848, along with seventy-seven other enslaved men, women and children, they secretly boarded the schooner *Pearl* and set sail for New Jersey and freedom—or so they thought. The tides and the wind were not in their favor, and a steamship sent by slaveholders captured and returned the fugitives to the city.[24]

The Pearl Incident, as it became known, was the largest recorded attempted escape of enslaved people in U.S. history. In response, supporters of slavery in Washington rioted for three days, targeting abolitionists and the free Black community. Emily and Mary were sold, along with the other attempted escapees, to traders and shipped to New Orleans. There, because of their youth and light skin, the slave traders Bruin and Hill displayed the sisters on a public porch, offering them as sex slaves for $1,200 each (nearly $50,000 in today's dollars). Only a yellow fever epidemic saved them from this fate: Bruin and Hill, to protect their investment, shipped them back north to Bruin's Slave Jail in Alexandria, Virginia.[25]

In the meantime, their father, Paul, had come to New York looking for help from the abolitionist community to save his daughters. He soon found Henry Ward Beecher, who used the girls' harrowing story to raise money for their release throughout the city. "How would you feel," he asked the congregation at the Broadway Tabernacle, "if your daughter were kidnapped and sold to a man who would rape her, sell her children for profit and whip her if she put up resistance?"[26] With this explicit and emotional appeal, Beecher raised the funds needed, and he personally traveled to Alexandria, where he bought the Edmonson sisters' freedom on November 4, 1848, nearly seven months after their ordeal began.

Above: Frederick Douglass (*seated, left of table*) with Mary and Emily Edmonson (*standing, in patterned shawls*) at the Fugitive Slave Convention in Cazenovia, New York, 1850. *Public domain.*

Left: Edmonson Sisters Memorial in Alexandria, Virginia, Erik Blome, 2010. *Bronzecastman.*

After reuniting with their family, the sisters moved to Cortland, New York, in 1850 to attend New York Central College with help from the parishioners of Plymouth Church. They went to abolitionist rallies, including one where they met and befriended Frederick Douglass. The sisters also participated in Beecher's mock slave auctions to raise money to free others from circumstances they knew all too well. Harriet Beecher Stowe, the sister of Henry Ward Beecher and the author of *Uncle Tom's Cabin*, published in 1852, later cited the Edmonson sisters' harrowing tale as one of the inspirations for her work.[27]

The fact that the story of the Edmonson sisters was seemingly ignored at the dedication of the Beecher memorial is unfortunate but not surprising. It was a day intended to glorify Beecher and the history of his great church. It also is not surprising that in the hierarchy of Borglum's piece, the girls were posed beneath the feet of the great man, as the young Black girl was in the John Quincy Adams Ward statue of Beecher. The subject of both statues was Beecher, and all other characters were in supporting roles. In fact, all other historical figures in the New York memorial landscape at that time were either white men alone or white men on horses. New Yorkers would have to wait an entire year to get their first monument to a female historical figure, until December 6, 1915, when a mounted statue of Joan of Arc by Anna Hyatt Huntington was dedicated in Riverside Park at Ninety-Third Street. As of this writing, New York boasts a paltry total of seven public monuments to real women: Joan of Arc, Gertrude Stein, Golda Meir, Eleanore Roosevelt, Harriet Tubman and Althea Gibson. The Women's Rights Pioneers Monument, dedicated in Central Park in 2020, includes three women: Sojourner Truth, Elizabeth Cady Stanton and Susan B. Anthony. A monument to Shirley Chisholm, the first woman to run for president, is planned for Prospect Park.

Those hoping for a more inspirational representation of Emily and Mary Edmonson can find one in Alexandria, Virginia, on the site of Bruin's Slave Jail, where they were once held. Dedicated in 2010, the Edmonson Sisters Memorial by Erik Blome is a heroic bronze statue featuring the sisters striding forward with their heads up, holding hands, appearing as they might have on the night they attempted to escape to freedom.

Chapter 7

MARQUIS DE LAFAYETTE MEMORIAL

Unveiling of the Marquis de Lafayette Memorial in 1917. *Library of Congress.*

SCULPTOR: Daniel Chester French (1850–1931)
DEDICATED: May 10, 1917
LOCATION: 9th Street, Prospect Park West
ARCHITECT: Henry Bacon
MATERIALS: Bronze and granite
SIZE: Bas-relief H × W: 10' × 13'
Stela H × W × D: 19' × 22' × 8'10"
Terrace W × D: 72' × 35'
DONOR: Henry Harteau

Inscription:

Front:

> *THE MARQUIS DE LAFAYETTE. THIS MONUMENT WAS ERECTED AND PRESENTED BY HENRY HARTEAU, A DISTINGUISHED CITIZEN OF BROOKLYN, TO BE AN ENDURING TRIBUTE TO THE MEMORY OF ONE WHO, AS A FRIEND AND COMPANION OF THE IMMORTAL WASHINGTON, FOUGHT TO ESTABLISH IN OUR COUNTRY THOSE VITAL PRINCIPLES OF LIBERTY AND HUMAN BROTHERHOOD WHICH HE AFTERWARD LABORED TO ESTABLISH IN HIS OWN.*

Rear:

> *THIS MEMORIAL WAS UNVEILED AND DEDICATED BY MARSHALL JOFFRE AND M. VIVANI OF THE FRENCH WAR COMMISSION, MAY 10, 1917.*

The Black man holding the horse in the Lafayette memorial appears to be jerking his head away from the testy mount of the dashing French hero of the American Revolution, the Marquis de Lafayette. Lafayette stands, sword drawn, hand on hip, coolly surveying the distance. Unlike most Black people in statues of this era, the man holding the horse is in uniform and wearing shoes, but like many Black people in statues of this era, he is in the background, and his identity is unclear. Who this man actually was—if he was, in fact, anyone in particular—seemed of no known concern to anyone until 2016, when an investigative reporter, Summer Brennan, wrote an article for *New York Magazine*, "The Invisible Black Man on a Prospect Park Statue." Brennan claimed that online research led her to believe the man was the famed Revolutionary War spy James Armistead Lafayette. But was he?

James Armistead Lafayette (1748–1830) was born into slavery as James Armistead in Virginia. He was the property of William Armistead, the military supply commissary for the Marquis de Lafayette during the Virginia campaign. In 1781, James, who could read and write, asked for and received Armistead's permission to serve the Marquis as a spy, hoping that his service would earn him freedom. James infiltrated the British ranks and became "a servant to Lord Cornwallis," according to a letter Lafayette sent to General Washington.[28] In this capacity as an attendant to the British commander, he

Clay model of the Marquis de Lafayette Memorial, part of Daniel Chester French's New York City Art Commission submission, 1916. *New York City Public Design Commission.*

provided intelligence on troop movements that helped the Americans win the decisive battle of the Revolution at Yorktown. To show his appreciation for James's extraordinary services, Lafayette, a committed abolitionist, wrote him a commendation meant for the eyes of the Virginia General Assembly. "James," Lafayette wrote, "has done essential services to me while I had the honour to command in this state. His intelligences from the enemy's camp were industriously collected and faithfully delivered."[29] Based on this remarkable letter, the State of Virginia granted James his freedom, and James showed his appreciation for the marquis by replacing his slave name, Armistead, with Lafayette.[30]

Lest we think too highly of the legislators' actions, James's emancipation was contingent on an assessment of his value so that the assembly could reimburse his owner, William Armistead, for his loss out of the state's "general fund."[31] All sentiment aside, James had been property, and his freedom was bought from his enslaver by the state in return for a service.

While it would be nice to believe that the man holding the horse in the Lafayette memorial is James Lafayette, there is little to no evidence to support this conclusion. The work was commissioned by Henry Harteau, a Brooklyn merchant of French descent with an outsized affection for his hero, Lafayette. He gifted the city $30,000 to make a statue based on *Lafayette at Yorktown* by Jean-Baptiste le Paon, a painting commissioned by Lafayette after the war showing him with a Black manservant holding his horse.[32] If the marquis intended for the Black man in the painting to be James, the man he relied on at Yorktown, there is no record of it. Likewise, James was not included in the memorial inscription, nor was he mentioned at the May 10, 1917 unveiling in Prospect Park, which was attended by thousands, including the commander in chief of the United States' French World War I allies, Marshal Joffre. Nor did he earn a comment in any of the reporting on the event and the statue. The memorial sculptor, Daniel Chester French, described him only as a "negro holding a horse."

The man is either an anonymous slave or a generic Black African, part of what Lafayette biographer Laura Aurricchio described as "a centuries-old tradition of picturing black grooms or pages in portraits of European noblemen." In *Lafayette at Yorktown*, the man in the bright red uniform with an earring and a fancy hat (an unlikely outfit for a spy) is only an accessory to complement a general, like his horse.[33] Accordingly, both the caption on an engraving of the painting, Noel Le Mire's *Conclusion de la Campagne de 1718 en Virginie*, and the extensive descriptive text sold with it make no mention of the man gripping Lafayette's horse.

The history of the early twentieth century in the United States also suggests that James was unlikely to be featured in a public statue. After all, this was a time when just one public monument in the nation, the Boston Massacre/Crispus Attucks Monument, dedicated three decades earlier in 1888, included a Black patriot of the Revolution. It was the height of Jim Crow, when Blacks were treated like second-class citizens. It was a time when adherents of the influential Dunning School, a racist view of Reconstruction named after a preeminent Columbia University history professor, argued, among other things, that giving Blacks the right to vote and hold office had been a mistake. And it was a time when President Woodrow Wilson hosted a screening of *The Birth of a Nation*, a film celebrating the Ku Klux Klan, in the White House. In 1915, the year of that infamous screening, W.E.B. Du Bois wrote this devastating critique of African American historiography:

Conclusion de la campagne de 1781 en Virginie, Noel Le Mire's engraving of Lafayette and groom, after Le Paon. *Library of Congress.*

> *In order to paint the South as a martyr to inescapable fate, to make the North the magnanimous emancipator, and to ridicule the Negro as the impossible joke in the whole development, we have in fifty years, by libel, innuendo and silence, so completely misstated and obliterated the history of the Negro in America and his relation to its work and government that today it is almost unknown.*[34]

Given Du Bois's assessment of the deplorable public image of Black people at the time, the idea of James being the Black man on the Lafayette memorial grows even more remote.

In the absence of proof, one is left to conclude that James Lafayette is not the other man in the Le Paon painting and, therefore, not the man holding the horse in the Lafayette memorial. So why not go along with the idea that he's James Lafayette? After all, it may not be him, but shouldn't it be? Or consider this: rather than reducing him to just the Black man holding the white man's horse, wouldn't a more fitting commemoration for one of the United States' greatest spies be a memorial of his own? At present, none exist, and there appear to be no plans for one. On the other end of Prospect Park from the Lafayette memorial, a well-deserved monument is planned to celebrate another great American, Shirley Chisholm, the first Black woman to run for president. Certainly, one of the United States' greatest spies deserves a similar tribute.

Chapter 8

COTTON, INDUSTRIES OF THE BRITISH EMPIRE

Cotton figure in *Industries of the British Empire*, Paul Jennewein, 1933. *David Jacobs.*

SCULPTOR: Carl Paul Jennewein
DEDICATED: April 4, 1933
LOCATION: British Empire Building, 620 5th Avenue, Rockefeller Center
ARCHITECT: Raymond Hood
MATERIALS: Gilded bronze relief
DONOR: Rockefeller Center

Inscription:

Dieu et Mon Droit

Swept along in Fifth Avenue's great current, you'd most likely miss her, but look above the doors of the old British Empire Building, and there she is: *Cotton*. Unveiled in 1933, she is one of nine gilded bronze figures celebrating the industries of the British Empire above a sun which, at least in this panel, never sets. The *New York Times* described this work as "one of Rockefeller Center's most successful essays in embellishment."[35] While the white sculptor, Carl Paul Jennewein, represented cotton with an African woman to celebrate the greatness and breadth of the British Empire, it's hard for the contemporary eye to see this shoeless, half-naked woman standing beside a cotton plant and a basket as anything but a reminder of Britain's reliance on slave labor. In the same way, his *Sugar* figure, which appears to be an Asian man, evokes the specter of labor coerced by the empire from Mumbai to Hong Kong.

Built against the odds in the midst of the Depression, Rockefeller Center is one of New York's great commercial centers. The sprawling midtown campus is the stage for dramatic statues, reliefs and murals all intending to tell the story of mankind's progress, from achievements in science, art and technology to the eternal quest for immortality. Naturally, the default race of the figures in these scenes was, almost without exception, white, as it was in almost all public sculpture in the United States in the 1930s. The epic future belonged to them, and the "negress among cotton plants" on the bottom rung at the British Empire Building is only there to support their achievements.[36] Despite the vibrant expressions of Black culture still emanating from the Harlem Renaissance at this time, there appears to be only one piece in all of Rockefeller Center that represents Black American contributions, and that's a Black saxophone player in one of Rene Paul Chambellin's six bronze plaques that make up *Acts of Vaudeville* on the walls at the entrance to Radio City Music Hall.

As for the artist, Jennewein's own thoughts about *Cotton* are unknown. What we do know is that the German-born American artist was perhaps best known for the scenes he inscribed on the columns at the entrance of the Central Branch of the Brooklyn Public Library in 1938. The classical figures of these gilded reliefs show the evolution of art and science, but as some critics have pointed out, Jennewein saved the civilizing roles for white characters here and gave the parts of slaves and laborers to non-whites at the

Industries of the British Empire above the entrance to the British Empire Building at Rockefeller Center. *David Jacobs.*

British Empire Building.[37] These choices could be dismissed as consistent with the times, but something more sinister was afoot: Jennewein's enthusiastic participation in Hitler's Great German Art Exhibitions in Munich from 1937 to 1939.

Jennewein's German heritage and his spare neoclassical style, with an emphasis on women in traditional roles as mothers or sexual objects, was consistent with the Nazi aesthetic, making him a welcome guest in Hitler's Munich. In a letter to a friend, he praised the attendance at and overall spirit of the event, claiming it was the "answer [to] what is wrong with American Art." Jennewein was there during Hitler's infamous Degenerate Art Exhibition of 1937, meant to show the superiority of classic "Aryan" art over "degenerate" modern art. Nobody visiting Germany at this time could have any doubts about Hitler's views on race and his plans for world domination. In 1938, Jennewein was singled out by *der führer* himself when he sold him three female nude bronzes for $87,000 (in today's dollars). Given his open admiration of Germany and German art, it should perhaps come as no surprise that his work at the Brooklyn Library and Rockefeller Center would be consistent with Nazi racist theories.[38]

Whatever Nazi sympathies the artist may have had, he appears to have been loyal to the United States, designing a Saint Christopher Medal for soldiers during World War II and, later, a medal honoring the twentieth anniversary of the Allied victory in Europe. Perhaps what's truly alarming is how typical racist attitudes and work like his were in the United States at that time. Consider, for example, the rally of the German American Bund at Madison Square Garden in 1939, just one year after Jennewein's Brooklyn Library work, or the countless Confederate monuments to Lost Cause heroes erected during the Jim Crow era. Both were clear, public statements of white supremacy very much in line with Hitler's racist beliefs.

Chapter 9

WOMAN, THE MOTHER AND HOUSEKEEPER AND *MAN, THE PROVIDER*

Left: *Woman, the Mother and Housekeeper*, Heinz Warneke, 1938. *Right*: *Man, the Provider*, Heinz Warneke, 1938. *National Archives*.

Sculptor: Heinz Warneke (1895–1983)
Dedicated: 1938
Location: Harlem River Houses
Architect: Archibald Manning Brown
Materials: Pink stone
Size: Each statue H: 6'
Donor: Treasury Relief Art Project (T.R.A.P.)

The members of the Harlem Housing Committee didn't like what they saw. The all-Black group found the model for the statue *Man, the Provider*, a Black worker naked from the waist up, offensive. Why couldn't he be dressed in a coat and tie like a businessman? The committee made up of prominent Harlem citizens, including NAACP leader Walter White, represented the future Black tenants of the Harlem River Houses, and this meeting took place just a year before the apartments were set to open, in 1937. It was the first federally subsidized housing project in New York City, and it was also built for a largely Black community. *Man, the Provider* and another statue, *Woman, the Mother and Housekeeper*, were slated to adorn the development's main courtyard.[39]

The committee arranged a meeting at the studio of the sculptor, Heinz Warneke, and invited a delegation of Black artists to consult. It was only after the artists explained to the committee that Warneke's choice to show the worker partially nude was common in art and that Warneke meant no disrespect that they accepted the concept. They did, however, have one lingering concern: the lips and the noses of both statues were too large. Warneke agreed to reduce the features but complained in a letter to a friend, "The two large negro figures are a bit 'modified' not as I should have chosen—the negro committee didn't want them too negroid!"[40] Warneke may have scoffed at the committee's critique, but decades before the embrace of the Black Is Beautiful movement, their response undoubtedly reflected a sensitivity to widespread racist caricatures of Black people.

Man, the Provider and *Woman, the Mother and Housekeeper* were the first public statues in New York City made to both represent and inspire a Black community. The Harlem River Houses, between 151st and 153rd Streets on the Harlem River, were groundbreaking themselves, an experiment in public housing built in response to overcrowding, poverty and crime. In 1935, the Black population of Harlem was roughly two hundred thousand, a 400 percent increase over the Black population of the entire city in 1910.[41] In fact, since 1920, Harlem had been the largest Black community in the United States. This incredible growth was caused by the Great Migration of African Americans fleeing violence in the Jim Crow South for the promise of economic and educational opportunities in the North. The Great Migration also fueled the cultural explosion of the Harlem Renaissance—for a lucky few. Most Blacks were confined to manual labor and excluded from white collar work. The Great Depression led to high unemployment in an overpopulated Harlem, where housing was already cramped, expensive and limited. In 1935, a race riot broke out, causing over $2 million in property

From left to right: Richmond Barthé, Theodore Barbarosa, Heinz Warneke and Steinberg (first name unknown) in 1939 in Warneke's studio at 5 Washington Mews. *Archives of American Art.*

damage and the deaths of three Black residents. In the riot's wake, Mayor Fiorello La Guardia's administration concluded that poor housing was a major cause of the violence. The city turned to the federal government for help.

In 1936, the Works Progress Administration, part of Franklin Roosevelt's New Deal, came through with a nearly $5 million federal subsidy to the New York City Housing Authority (NYCHA) for the construction of the Harlem River Houses. The project consisted of seven four- to five-story redbrick apartment buildings that looked out onto courtyards, playgrounds and gardens. One of the designers was John Louis Wilson, the first Black graduate of Columbia Architecture School. When tenants began moving in in the fall of 1937, the *New Amsterdam News* ran a full-page spread showing happy families seated in clean apartments with working kitchens and bathrooms, a vast improvement from the dirty, substandard slum apartments Harlem had become known for.[42] Of the project, Wilson later said, "We tried to create a humane architecture."[43] To this day, the Harlem River Houses are considered a model for progressive public housing and studied by urban planners around the world.

With the Harlem River Houses, the federal government not only supported "humane architecture" but also, as was common with New Deal programs, public art. In this case, the Treasury Relief Art Project (TRAP) required that 1 percent of funds set aside for federal housing should go to "artistic decoration." New York's current Percent for Art Program to integrate art into public spaces was inspired in part by the TRAP funding model. To make the statues for the Harlem River Houses, the project's designers chose German-born sculptor Heinz Warneke. Warneke, best known for his evocative stone carvings of animals, like Penn State's Nittany Lion, put together a small team of artists, including one of the best-known Black sculptors of his time, Richmond Barthé. The team worked for over two years in Warneke's Washington Mews studio in Greenwich Village. The realistic *Man, the Provider* kneels with a hammer in his right hand and a gear, symbolizing industrial labor, resting between his knees. *Woman, the Mother and Housekeeper* is crouching and holding her child as the family dog looks on. The six-foot-tall statues were made to look out over the main courtyard from the north and south entrances, and Warneke had them cast in pink stone to match the brick of the apartments. During this time, the artists also produced four black stone penguin statues for a fountain in the courtyard and some playfully wrestling bears for the garden.[44] Barthé focused much of his energies on creating an eighty-foot-wide bas-relief of a Black exodus to the promised land based on the Pulitzer Prize–winning Broadway play *The Green Pastures*. Barthé's bas-relief was intended for a planned amphitheater at the Harlem River Houses that was never built. Instead, the monumental piece was placed in Brooklyn's Kingsborough Houses in 1941 (to learn more, see page 62).

In 1938, when *Man, the Provider* and *Woman, the Mother and Housekeeper* were installed, critics approved of both the process by which the pieces were made and their aesthetics. A 1938 *Art Magazine* article claimed that "government art projects" like Harlem River Houses, "with their extensive use of committees representing the public, have revolutionized patronage." While most public statues in New York to this point had been funded by private money or public subscription, committees of almost entirely elite white citizens made decisions about the subject, design and location. Here, for the first time in New York City, were public statues of Black people funded by the federal government with input from elite citizens of the Black community, for the Black community. *Art Magazine* described the shirtless and kneeling man as "dignified," adding that both statues were informed by a "clear vision and intelligent study."[45] Tenants embraced the works as well. Many photos from the time showed adults admiring them and children climbing on them. According to the *New Amsterdam News*, "The strength of the provider is seen in his tremendous physical prowess. The family is represented by the mother and child and the homelike contentment of their faithful dog."[46] These groundbreaking works were intended and received as heroic representations of a Black man and a Black woman, larger than life, on pedestals in a Black neighborhood. At the time, they were the only statues fitting that description in New York City.

Chapter 10

EXODUS AND DANCE MONUMENT

Right panel in *Exodus and Dance*, Richmond Barthé, 1941. *David Jacobs.*

SCULPTOR: Richmond Barthé (1901–1989)
DEDICATED: 1941
LOCATION: Kingsborough Houses, Crown Heights
ARCHITECT: N/A
MATERIALS: Stone bas-relief
SIZE: Frieze H × W: 8' × 80'
DONOR: Treasury Relief Art Project

Question: What's made of stone, eighty feet wide and in the wrong place? Answer: *Exodus and Dance* by Richmond Barthé. Since 1941, this monumental sixteen-panel frieze has dominated the central plaza of Brooklyn's Kingsborough Houses, but it was originally intended for the Harlem River Houses. Barthé, one of the few African Americans making sculpture for the public in the city at that time, was excited by the prospect of designing specifically for the Black community in Harlem. Given the task of decorating the outer wall of a planned amphitheater, he spent nearly two years crafting a giant relief only to learn soon after finishing that the amphitheater would not be built and, until another location could be found for it, the New York City Housing Authority (NYCHA) was putting the relief in storage.

Despite his disappointment, Barthé had plenty of work to keep him busy. One of the greatest sculptors of his age, he completed at least forty pieces a year, according to the *New Amsterdam News*. In 1938, he made busts of John Gielgud, Gypsy Lee Rose and Paul Robeson.[47] Barthé, born in Mississippi, showed a talent for drawing at an early age, discovered sculpture while studying at the Art Institute of Chicago and moved to Harlem in 1929. The talented and attractive Barthé soon established himself as an important artist.[48] In 1931, Alain Locke, the intellectual father of the Harlem Renaissance, listed Barthé in a roll call of Black artists including Paul Robeson, Langston Hughes and Marian Anderson. "These artists," wrote Locke, "are in the first flush of creative conquest of the formal arts; they rightly feel themselves to be the first generation of true Negro artists."[49] But while Barthé was part of the Harlem Renaissance, he wanted to be known as more than just a Black artist. "I don't think that art is racial," he said in a 1931 *New York Times* interview, "but I do feel that a Negro can portray the inner feelings of the Negro people better than a white man can."[50] Outraged by the rise in lynchings in the 1930s, he created *The Mother* (1935), inspired by Michelangelo's *Pieta*, which depicts a young Black victim of a lynching lying in the arms of his grieving mother.[51]

Sculptor Richmond Barthé at work in his Harlem studio in the 1920s or '30s, from film *Study of Negro Artists*, in the Prelinger Archives. *Public domain.*

Exodus and Dance, Richmond Barthé, 1941. *David Jacobs.*

For the Harlem River Houses, Barthé again focused on Black subjects, but in this case, he chose an uplifting scene inspired by the Pulitzer Prize–winning Broadway play *The Green Pastures*. The drama, by white playwright Marc Connelly, imagined an all-Black heaven with a Black God, "De Lawd," decidedly in charge of both heaven and earth. Not only popular with Black audiences, it was adapted for the screen in 1938, the same time Barthé began working on the relief for the Harlem River Houses. Inspired by Egyptian tomb murals in the Metropolitan Museum, the left panel of *Exodus and Dance* shows an ancient, stooped Moses, leaning on his brother Aaron, leading a column of Black Israelites out of slavery to the promised land of freedom and open spaces—in this case, the Harlem River Houses. The right panel was not inspired by *The Green Pastures* but sprang, rather, from the artist's imagination. It represents two lines of women dancing in unison, their attention drawn to three men at the center of the action. A drummer seated to the left drives the scene. Barthé had imagined his frieze welcoming generations of Black Harlemites to open-air performances of Zora Neale Hurston's plays or readings of Langston Hughes's poems and was upset to learn in 1941 that the government had put his work in the Kingsborough Houses in the Brooklyn neighborhood of Crown Heights.

Both Barthé and Black people in Crown Heights were disappointed to find that, as the *New York Age* reported, the first wave of residents in the Kingsborough Houses was majority white, despite it being a majority Black neighborhood. This fueled Black resentment of a citywide phenomenon: whites moving into Black neighborhoods to take advantage of cheaper housing. Despite these concerns, within a few decades, Kingsborough became more than two-thirds Black. Barthé, however, was still apparently so upset by the location of his work that he refused to help when renovations became necessary.[52]

By 2018, the condition of *Exodus and Dance* had deteriorated to the point where the cast stone was cracking, and some feared the entire structure could collapse. Alarmed by the state of such a valuable piece of heritage, Art historian Michele Bogart began tweeting about her concerns and tagging Chirlane McCray, then New York City's First Lady and an influential force for public art during the DeBlasio administration.[53] The tweets drew the attention of the city council, which allocated $1.8 million for the renovation of the piece. In January 2024, NYCH removed it from the site for preservation, as of this writing, it is expected to return in 2025.

Chapter 11

COLONEL WILLIAM HAYWARD MEMORIAL PLAQUE

Colonel William Hayward memorial plaque, Selma Burke, 1945. *Author photo.*

SCULPTOR: Selma Burke
DEDICATED: September 30, 1945
LOCATION: 369th Regiment Armory, Harlem New York (2366 5th Avenue)
MATERIALS: Bronze
DONOR: Public subscription

Inscription:

> *IN MEMORIAM: COL. WILLIAM HAYWARD; OFFICERS AND MEN, 15TH NEW YORK INFANTRY U.S. A.E.F.*
>
> *FAMOUS FIRSTS*
>
> *ONLY VOLUNTEER REGIMENT RAISED FOR THE WAR WHICH REACHED FRANCE*
>
> *EMBARKED AS PART OF FIRST 100,000 A.E.F.*
>
> *SHIPWRECKED THREE TIMES ENROUTE* [SIC] *TO FRANCE*
>
> *ONLY REGIMENT IN HISTORY OF U.S. TO SERVE AS AN INTEGRAL PART OF A FOREIGN ARMY*
>
> *FIRST AMERICAN PRIVATES IN ARMY OF FRANCE TO RECEIVE CROIX DE GUERRE: HENRY JOHNSON, NEEDHAM ROBERTS*
>
> *REGIMENT CITED BY FRENCH HIGH COMMAND APPROVED BY AMERICAN HIGH COMMAND FOR EXTRAORDINARY GALLANTRY IN ACTION AND COLORS DECORATED WITH CROIX DE GUERRE*
>
> *FIRST REGIMENT OF THE ALLIES TO REACH THE RHINE*
>
> *SERVED 191 DAYS IN ACTION, LONGEST OF ANY AMERICAN REGIMENT*
>
> *NEVER LOST A MAN BY CAPTURE OR A FOOT OF GROUND*
>
> *FIRST COMBAT REGIMENT TO ARRIVE HOME AND TO MARCH UP FIFTH AVENUE UNDER THE VICTORY ARCH*

Some American soldiers returned from World War I hoping for honors more enduring than parades, and memorial statues were one way their service and sacrifice would be remembered for generations to come. In 1919, the painter Cecile Beaux, writing in the *American Magazine of Art* about the purpose of war memorials, asked,

> *What will best lead* [the average mind] *to the moment of seriousness, the real consciousness of the young life fallen in its prime, and never more to see the sun, the consciousness of the sacrifice for our good, and what we owe it of eternal memory, from generation to generation?*
>
> *Surely the most poignant reminder must be the image of the boy himself, as he goes to the front, with the burden of his full kit, and accoutrement from under which his boyish, lean, American face, looks.*[54]

As if in response to Beaux's recommendation, hundreds of realistic bronze monuments of soldiers, known as doughboy statues, spread across the country in the years following the war. While many such memorials appeared in New York's white neighborhoods (at that time), like Woodside, Queens, Red Hook, Brooklyn and Chelsea in Manhattan, they remained conspicuously absent from the city's Black communities.

Of the nearly five million American men who served in World War I, over 350,000 were Black.[55] President Woodrow Wilson took the country to war saying that "the world must be made safe for democracy." And even though the benefits of American democracy were mostly for whites, many Black Americans still served. Perhaps they served because W.E.B. Du Bois had famously argued that Germany was a greater threat to their "equality" and "freedom" than their "white fellow citizens." Or they served because, like many before them, they saw fighting for their country as a way to gain rights, recognition and respect. But if the memorial landscape of the country after the war was any indication, not much had changed.

In fact, according to the United States World War I Centennial Commission, there are thousands of public memorials in the United States dedicated to the men, and some women, who served and gave their lives in the war.[56] But out of all these, there appear to be only three completed by the end of World War II in which the images of Black soldiers appear: the All Wars Memorial to Colored Soldiers and Sailors in Philadelphia, Chicago's Victory Monument and the Colonel Hayward Memorial Plaque in New York. The latter included the famed Fifteenth Regiment of New York, made up of Black soldiers, widely known as the Harlem Hellfighters.

This is how the editorial page of the *New York Tribune* described the Black troops of the Fifteenth in February 1919 on their return from Europe after World War I:

> *The bass* [sic] *relief of the Shaw Memorial became a living thing as the dusky heroes of the 15th cheered the Liberty Statue and happily swarmed down the gangplank. Appropriately the arrival was on the birthday of the blessed Massa Abraham.*[57]

The column reveals the white newspaper's mixed feelings about Black soldiers. On the one hand, they're "heroes," who fought and won the Great War; on the other, nearly fifty years after emancipation, they're still trapped in the past, seen as beholden to "Massa Abraham." The article also evokes two famous American statues: the Statue of Liberty and the Memorial to Robert Gould Shaw and the Fifty-Fourth Massachusetts Regiment. The former, dedicated in 1886, was a symbol of liberty and friendship between France and the United States that came to be known as a beacon for immigrants. The latter, unveiled in Boston in 1897, commemorated the Civil War service of Captain Shaw and the Black soldiers of the Fifty-Fourth who fought to end slavery and preserve the Union.

The unveiling of these two monuments toward the end of the nineteenth century might lead one to believe that the values of equality, justice and liberty were celebrated in that United States, but in 1919, even this *Tribune* editorial recognized the dissonance of Black American men cheering a statue dedicated to liberty:

> *The boys cheered the Bartholdi statue. It makes the white man uncomfortable. It converts into strange reading glib eulogies of democratic principles. The success of one our chief political parties is predicated on suppression of the negro vote.*[58]

The Black soldiers who cheered the Statue of Liberty on that February day lived in a segregated country and had all experienced racism in and out of the service. They understood that the nation they had just fought, bled and died for in appalling numbers was falling short of its promise, and still they cheered.

New York's Fifteenth "Colored" Infantry Regiment, Harlem's Rattlers, marching on Fifth Avenue in 1919. *New York Public Library.*

A few days after cheering Lady Liberty, New York's Fifteenth found themselves marching, sixteen men abreast, up Manhattan's Fifth Avenue to the music of their regimental band, directed by James Reese Europe, the man who introduced jazz to Europe. Today, these men are known as Harlem's Hellfighters, but the name they chose for themselves was Harlem's Rattlers, in reference to their unit insignia: a rattlesnake, taken from the Revolutionary War Gadsden flag with the motto "Don't tread on me."[59] Their commander, Colonel William Hayward, a white attorney and advisor to New York Governor Seymour Whitman, had a reputation for treating his Black soldiers fairly.[60] Led by Black and white officers, the Rattlers, renamed the 369th in France, endured 191 days in combat, more than any other U.S. regiment. They were the first Americans to cross the Rhine into Germany and won a regimental Croix de Guerre citation from the French High Command for gallantry.

The Rattlers famously "never lost a man by capture or a foot of ground."[61] But at the request of President Wilson's blatantly racist administration, they were excluded from triumphal marches in Paris after the war.[62] Even in celebrating victory, the government was intent on reminding Blacks of their place in society. In that vein, it would not have been lost on the men that no white regiments joined them that day in New York. The United States' victory celebrations, like its military, would be segregated.

The first concrete recognition of the Rattlers' service in New York was the monumental Harlem Armory, a brick, medieval-looking drill shed built by the firm of Tachau and Vought in 1927. The building, with three levels of balconies that could seat up to seven thousand, served as a headquarters and training facility for the regiment and as an entertainment arena for the public. Today, it remains the base of the 369th Sustainment Brigade and home to community athletic and academic programs. At the time, veterans of the Rattlers were thrilled to have their own armory, but they and members of their community still hoped for some greater recognition for their service.[63]

In the years before and after World War I, negative depictions of Blacks in American media were all too common—like the recently, and thankfully, retired Aunt Jemima. This caricature, based on a minstrel character and song, had been on boxes of pancake mix since 1889.[64] *Birth of a Nation*, a popular film famously screened at Wilson's White House, portrayed Blacks as subhuman and the Ku Klux Klan as heroes. Because of the proliferation of racist characterizations like these, the lack of public images that depicted African Americans as competent, even heroic, human beings was glaring. But the wait for such images in war memorials would be long.

In April 1928, a Black "civic worker" from Harlem, Esther Archer, wrote a letter to a Black paper, the *New York Age*, in which she proposed constructing a "monument to commemorate the bravery of the negro soldiers in the late great war" in a small Harlem park named for Dorrence Brooks, a private killed fighting with the Rattlers in France. Archer wanted a memorial that would demonstrate what she described as "our group's contributions to humanity." She envisioned a monument with "a quadrangle base, typifying educational achievement, music, poetry, etc.," and displaying the names of famous Black men like Booker T. Washington, James Reese Europe and the poet Paul Lawrence Dunbar. Atop the pedestal would be "a commanding military figure by Miss Augusta Savage or some other race sculptor."

Archer's vision was typical of what many communities hoped to get from a doughboy memorial: a place to honor their fallen, a focal point for civic activities, and an inspiring symbol of "commanding" manhood, which, in this case, happened to be Black. Archer's proposed inscription for the memorial also shows how she, like many other Black Americans, felt the nation had failed to adequately reward Black people for their service: "We gave all for our country," Archer wrote. "Will she give to our people protection and equal opportunity?"[65]

Archer's vision was never realized. Getting a memorial built was and remains a complicated, expensive process that requires political and community support. It would have been challenging under any circumstances, but it's possible the Great Depression put Archer's memorial out of reach. It wasn't until after World War II that the Rattlers would get a memorial in Harlem, but it was a long way from Esther Archer's grand vision.

So what did it finally take to get the Rattlers memorialized in bronze in Harlem over a quarter-century after they returned from France? The death of their white commander. In the fall of 1944, Colonel William Hayward, beloved by the Black soldiers of the 369th, died at age sixty-seven. Over sixty veterans of the 369th formed the honor guard for his funeral casket. His obituary in the *Age* had nothing but praise: "His career…was studded with service to the cause of Negro rights….His was not a paternalistic service, but a sympathetic and sincere desire to help bring about full democracy for the Negro." The Veterans Association of the 369th quickly rallied to raise the money and commissioned a memorial.[66]

On September 30, 1945, a reported sixteen thousand people filled the sidewalks of Harlem to watch three thousand soldiers and veterans of the 369th march to the Harlem Armory, where they were joined by First Lady Eleanor Roosevelt, civil rights activist Mary Mcleod Bethune and Mayor

Colonel William Hayward training in a U.S. trench in 1917. *National Archives.*

Fiorello La Guardia for the unveiling of a bronze tablet honoring Colonel Hayward and the officers and men of the 369th. The plaque was the work of Black sculptor Selma Burke, who had recently completed a plaque of President Roosevelt in profile for the Office of Deeds. The piece at the armory was based on a painting by S.J. Woolf, *The First to the Rhine*, showing the Rattlers marching under the watchful eye of Colonel Hayward. In her My Day column on the event, Eleanor Roosevelt took time to remind her readers of the heroism of the Black soldiers, "who fought and made a brilliant record in the first World War."[67]

While the First Lady kindly highlighted the achievements of the Black soldiers in the 369th, a closer look at the memorial reveals the subject of the piece to be Colonel Hayward, clearly identifiable in the foreground while his Black soldiers march in the background. One Black soldier carries a guitar in addition to his rifle, and another looks toward Hayward, but other than that, each man is indistinguishable from the next. While the tablet reads "In Memoriam; Col. William Hayward; Officers and Men, 15th New York Infantry" and lists the "Famous Firsts" of the regiment, there is no mention of them being Black troops. The headline of the *New York Times* piece about the ceremony said simply, "Plaque to Haywood Unveiled by Widow." Despite the impressive turnout and the celebration of the achievements of the 369th, rather than the heroic doughboy memorial in a public square that Esther Archer had in mind, the Rattlers were relegated to a semipublic military facility and practically hidden in the background of a tablet featuring their white commander.

The Rattlers would have to wait over half a century to be distinctly honored as a regiment in New York. Dedicated on September 29, 2006, the 369th Infantry Regiment Memorial is a dignified black obelisk located in a small park outside the Harlem Armory on Fifth Avenue, made possible by the 369th Historical Society and other donors. It is a replica of a 1997 monument dedicated in the village of Sechault, northern France, scene of Rattler heroics during the Meuse-Argonne offensive of 1918. The memorial tablet to Colonel Haywood remains on the wall just inside the entrance to the Armory across the street. It is not easily accessible to the public.

Chapter 12

BOOKER T. WASHINGTON MONUMENT

Booker T. Washington bust, Richmond Barthé. *David Jacobs.*

SCULPTOR: Richmond Barthé (1901–1989)
DEDICATED: May 23, 1946
LOCATION: Hall of Fame for Great Americans, Bronx Community College, 2155 University Avenue and West 181st Street, Bronx, New York 10453
ARCHITECT: Stanford White
MATERIALS: Bronze
DONOR: Tuskegee Institute and Hampton Institute

Inscription:

> *1858–1915, BOOKER T. WASHINGTON: THE HIGHEST TEST OF THE CIVILIZATION OF A RACE IS ITS WILLINGNESS TO EXTEND A HELPING HAND TO THE LESS FORTUNATE.*

In the spring of 1946, the unveiling of Booker T. Washington's bust at the Hall of Fame for Great Americans in the Bronx drew over one thousand people. The celebrations included music by the Tuskegee Institute Choir and an interpretive dance telling the story of Dr. Washington's life by the Hampton Institute Creative Dance Group. A letter from President Harry Truman was read, which said in part: "Now he is numbered among the immortal Americans in the Hall of Fame. In the years to come he will be an inspiration to every American who forges ahead despite the obstacles of his birth."[68] Both the Black and white press made much of the fact that Washington was the first Black American elected to the shrine, that the Tuskegee and Hampton Institutes had raised $5,000 (more than $85,000 today) for the bust and that the artist, Richmond Barthé, was the first Black sculptor to have his work included in the hall. Unremarked on was the fact that Washington was the first real Black person to have a public statue erected in his honor in New York City. Up until that moment, Black people had been featured only as symbolic figures in the city's memorial landscape.

To some, Booker Taliaferro Washington was a logical choice for the hall. Born into slavery just before the Civil War, he fell in love with reading after emancipation in 1865 and worked his way from janitor to professor at Virginia's Hampton Institute. He founded the Tuskegee Institute in Alabama in 1881 and, later, the National Negro Business League. Washington believed that the best way for Blacks to thrive in a segregated society was by learning trades like brickmaking and blacksmithing and by developing character traits like cleanliness and industriousness.[69] He dedicated his life to promoting both Black education and Black businesses throughout the country. His White House dinner with President Roosevelt was a first for a Black American, and his autobiography, *Up from Slavery*, was widely read.

To others, Booker T. was an "Uncle Tom" who aimed too low for Black people. At the 1895 Atlanta Exposition, he infamously told a mostly white audience that Blacks didn't want social equality, just economic opportunity: "In all things that are purely social we can be as separate as the fingers, yet one as the hand in all things essential to mutual progress."[70] This seeming acceptance of segregation earned him the enmity of Black leaders like

Sculptor Richmond Barthé (*left*) and Frank Totton, national campaign chair of the United Negro College Fund, with bust of Booker T. Washington. *Bronx Community College Archives.*

W.E.B. Du Bois, and major Black papers like the *Pittsburgh Courier* openly questioned Booker T.'s selection to the hall. Former slave and civil rights leader Frederick Douglass had also been in the running for the hall in 1945, and the *Courier* argued his leadership in the abolition movement and his tireless fight for the Black vote made him a better choice. "He was," according to the *Courier*, "more on the Negro's side" than Washington. So why Washington and not Douglass? The answer lies in the story of the Hall of Fame itself.

Before there was the Baseball Hall of Fame (1936), there was the Hall of Fame for Great Americans. Founded in 1900 on what was then the Bronx campus of New York University (now Bronx Community College), it was the idea of NYU Chancellor Henry MacCracken, who wished to celebrate remarkable Americans. Inspired by Munich's Ruhmeshalle (Hall of Fame), Westminster Abbey and Paris's Pantheon, the hall is an outdoor colonnade designed by the architect Stanford White. Part of the Gould Memorial Library, it rests on the highest point in the Bronx, overlooking the Harlem River, and holds 102 busts of American politicians, artists, scientists, writers, soldiers and educators. Only 11 white women, 2 Black men and 1 Jew are among them. There are no Catholics or Muslims.[71] In its inaugural year, the hall admitted 27 honorees, including George Washington, Abraham Lincoln and Robert E. Lee.[72] The installation of George Washington Carver's bust, also by Barthé, in 1977 (see page 99) made him the only African American resident besides Booker T. The hall's final selection to receive a statue was Franklin Delano Roosevelt, in 1992. Elections to the hall were once followed

Right: Booker T. Washington, undated portrait. *New York Public Library*.

Below: Bust of Booker T. Washington in the colonnade of the Hall of Fame for Great Americans. *Author photo*.

with great interest in the national press, and tourists flocked to the remote campus to admire its "Great Americans."

To qualify for the hall, one had to be a U.S. citizen, have lived in the United States and have been dead for at least twenty-five years. The hall's founder, Chancellor MacCracken, established a democratic selection process that relied on the public to send nomination letters to the NYU Senate. The senate forwarded names deemed appropriate to a group of one hundred electors, prominent citizens from around the country: university presidents, politicians, historians, scientists, Supreme Court justices, artists and journalists. MacCracken hoped that this national body would represent the "wisdom of the American People."[73] Beginning in 1900, the hall held so-called quinquennial elections (every five years), and nominations receiving a simple majority of votes were selected, generally four or five per election. Each elector could vote for as many nominees as they liked, and campaigns for candidates were not uncommon. As late as 1965, Desirée Lucille Franklin, an elderly native of Georgia living on the Upper West Side of Manhattan, was actively lobbying electors for her Great American, Confederate President Jefferson Davis. An honorary president of the United Daughters of the Confederacy, Franklin was confident she would get her man in the hall. And with good reason: in 1955, she cochaired a successful campaign for another hero of the Lost Cause, General Stonewall Jackson.[74]

The campaign for Frederick Douglass began in 1920 when a Black NYU student, Cleveland G. Allen, sent a letter nominating him to the hall. After college, Allen became a journalist and, for a time, worked on Booker T. Washington's publicity staff. Allen, a lifelong devotee of the hall who saw it as an inspiration to young people, led an annual pilgrimage to the bust of Harriet Beecher Stowe, the abolitionist author of *Uncle Tom's Cabin*. Despite Allen's efforts, the support of the NAACP and other national Black organizations, the bid to put Douglass in the hall failed to take hold. In 1935, he received just three votes. In the 1940 election, Booker T. Washington, who died in 1915, became eligible for the hall; he received fifty-seven votes to Douglass's eight but fell just short of making the hall. In 1945, Washington received the most votes out of 130 nominees (fifty-seven) and was admitted, along with Thomas Paine, Walter Reed and the poet Sidney Lanier. Douglass received no votes.[75] Because the Hall of Fame ballot was secret, it's difficult to say exactly which of the electors chose Washington and not Douglass and why. One is left to infer their reasons from the overall voting records of the body.

Out of the 101 eligible electors in 1945, 88 were men and 13 were women. All of them were white, and many were from the South. It seems likely that the outspoken Douglass was simply too radical for most white people. The less confrontational Washington may have represented the kind of Black man these electors and most white Americans were more comfortable with. This is likely why, in 1940, the U.S. Postal Service made him the first Black man to grace a postage stamp.[76] No such honor was conferred on Douglass until 1967. Another indication of the racial attitudes of the electors who chose Booker T. Washington was their election on the same ballot of the poet and musician Sidney Lanier of Macon, Georgia. Lanier served in the Confederate army and died young of tuberculosis, which he contracted in a Union prison camp. Adopted as a symbol of the Lost Cause by the Daughters of the Confederacy, he became known as the Poet of the Confederacy for his idealized vision of the antebellum South. It seems reasonable to assume that a group with such obvious Lost Cause leanings was unlikely to support an agitator like Douglass instead of or in addition to the more accommodating Booker T. Washington. Despite the efforts of Allen and others, Douglass was never elected to the hall, and it wasn't until 2011 that New York City erected a statue in his honor on 110th Street and 8th Avenue near Central Park (to learn more, see page 155).

It is worth mentioning that Jefferson Davis never was elected to the hall either, and Confederates Robert E. Lee and Stonewall Jackson were removed in 2017 in the wake of the white supremacist rally in Charlottesville, Virginia.

Chapter 13

LINCOLN AND CHILD MONUMENT

Lincoln and Child, Charles Keck, 1949. *David Jacobs.*

SCULPTOR: Charles Keck (1875–1951)
DEDICATED: February 12, 1949
LOCATION: Lincoln Houses, 2120–2122 Madison Avenue, New York, New York 10037
MATERIALS: Bronze
DONOR: New York City Housing Authority

On February 12, 1949, the 140th anniversary of Abraham Lincoln's birthday was celebrated widely in New York City. Boy Scouts from Troop 472 in Kips Bay laid a wreath by the statue of Lincoln in Union Square. At the Harlem branch of the New York Public Library, the children's reading hour was devoted to learning about the Great Emancipator. Residents at the Abraham Lincoln Houses in Harlem, and their curious children, pressed forward to see a recently unveiled bronze statue, then called *Lincoln and Boy* (now *Lincoln and Child*). One child mounted the statue, it seems, to get a closer look at the boy, not Lincoln. Perhaps he wanted to make sure that the rare sight of a Black child like himself portrayed in bronze was actually real.[77]

Lincoln was famously fond of young people, and the sculptor, Charles Keck, had done a number of studies for a statue of the president and his son Tad but never received a commission for that concept. For the Lincoln Houses, Keck replaced Tad with an African American boy who, according to *New York Times* coverage of the unveiling, "struck [his] 'fancy' while posing for another work. The image of Lincoln embracing a young Black boy was intended to celebrate both emancipation and slum clearance in Harlem, a clearance that had culminated in the construction of affordable apartment buildings like the Lincoln Houses.

The New York City Housing Authority (NYCHA) developed the project, and its chairman, retired Major General Thomas Farrell, told the crowd that Lincoln "would be pleased to see that his statue has been placed, not in marble halls among the great but right in the middle of a recreation area, next to the small children's playground." Deputy Mayor John J. Bennet acknowledged that the city government had taken too long to improve Harlem housing and said the most fitting way to dedicate a statue to Lincoln would be to find "decent homes for everyone." Presumably, the 1,286 families living in the project, most of them African American, were a good start.[78]

It's not exactly clear how or why NYCHA chose the sculptor Charles Keck, but he was eminently qualified for the job. Born in New York City in 1875, the child of German immigrants, Keck trained at the National Academy of Design and, later, the Art Students' League. After a five-year apprenticeship with Augustus Saint-Gaudens, Keck studied at the American Academy in Rome for a number of years before returning to New York in 1905 to establish a studio at 148 West Thirty-Sixth Street, where he would work for the rest of his life.[79]

Keck was known for his realistic figurative statues of notable Americans throughout the United States. In 1922, his figure of Booker T. Washington was dedicated at the Tuskegee Institute in Alabama, just one year after his equestrian statue of General Stonewall Jackson was dedicated in Charlottesville, Virginia. The fact that neither Keck nor the Tuskegee Institute seemed bothered by the irony of sculpting a Confederate hero one year and a former slave dedicated to uplifting Black Americans the next is remarkable. Charlottesville removed Keck's Jackson memorial in 2021.

Chapter 14

COAST GUARD MEMORIAL

Coast Guard Memorial, Norman M. Thomas, 1955. *David Jacobs.*

SCULPTOR: Norman M. Thomas (1915–1986)
DEDICATED: May 30, 1955 (completed in 1947)
LOCATION: Battery Park
MATERIALS: Bronze and Deer Isle granite
SIZE: Group H: 8'10"
  Pedestal H × W × D: 5'8" × 5'3" × 3'4"
DONOR: United States Coast Guard and individual donors

INSCRIPTION:

> *IN MEMORY OF THE MEN AND WOMEN OF THE UNITED STATES COAST GUARD WHO SERVED THEIR COUNTRY IN WORLD WAR II A.D. 1941–1945.*

On January 8, 1945, the USS *Callaway* was en route to Luzon in the Philippines when it was attacked by Japanese kamikaze aircraft. The *Callaway*, part of the United States' Pacific Island–hopping campaign to roll back the gains of the Japanese Empire and conquer Japan itself, was an attack transport, with a Coast Guard crew of nearly six hundred officers and enlisted men armed with guns and cannons. As the Japanese pilots swung in, the *Callaway*'s gunners, including some Black guardsmen, downed two with 20- and 40-millimeter antiaircraft fire, but a third kamikaze broke through, striking the starboard side of the ship and the brave gunners who kept firing as the plane hurtled toward them. Seven men were instantly killed by the plane's impact, and many more died horrible deaths as fire driven by aircraft fuel erupted from the site of the crash. Twenty-three men in all were killed in the attack, one of the U.S. Coast Guard's worst losses of life during the war.

As it happened, the man who conceived of and sculpted the Coast Guard Memorial was aboard the *Callaway* and witnessed the heroism of the Black gunners. Norman Millet Thomas, a native of Maine, graduated from the Portland School of Fine Art (now Maine College of Art) in 1933 and studied at the National Academy of Design in New York and the American Academy in Rome. In 1942, shortly after Pearl Harbor, he enlisted in the Coast Guard and was designated a combat artist, one of a select group of men, including the artist Jacob Lawrence, who, in addition to risking their lives fulfilling their regular duties, were tasked with drawing and painting the war.[80] Prior to his mission in the Pacific, Thomas had completed a tour in the Atlantic as part of the Coast Guard's Greenland Patrol, and his paintings were featured in *Life* magazine.

During World War II, all branches of the service, like U.S. society, were officially segregated, but the Coast Guard and the Navy, because of the close quarters on ships, were more integrated. Still, Black men were allowed to serve only as stewards, cooks or mess attendants, positions with no petty officer status, meaning they held no rank over enlisted men. However, in combat, they could man guns, like the guardsmen on the *Callaway*.

Despite the damage inflicted by the kamikaze attack, the *Callaway* continued to Luzon and offloaded its troops. Norman Thomas went ashore

The sketch that inspired the Coast Guard Memorial: *The Road Back from Luzon*, by Norman M. Thomas, 1945. *National Archives.*

to draw the action. Among the many sketches he made was one of two white members of the Coast Guard party helping a wounded white soldier toward medical attention: *The Road Back from Luzon.* Thomas would later say that he based the Coast Guard Memorial on this sketch because the composition of the trio translated well to sculpture and its spirit represented the Coast Guard's lifesaving mission, "the great humanitarian work of our service in both peace and war."[81]

In July 1945, shortly before the end of the war in the Pacific, Thomas was stationed at the Coast Guard District Office in New York City. Acting on his own initiative, he proposed the concept of a Coast Guard memorial based on the sketch he made in Luzon. His superiors approved the idea, and in September that year, established a committee to raise money through small donations from members of the Coast Guard. The committee chose Battery Park as the site for the memorial because New York was known as the Cradle of the Coast Guard: it was founded there in 1790 by Alexander Hamilton, then secretary of the treasury.[82] New York City Mayor Fiorello La Guardia and Parks Commissioner Robert Moses both supported the project, which would cost an estimated $25,000 (nearly $350,000 today). Moses promised space for the memorial in Battery Park on completion of the Brooklyn Battery Tunnel.

Thomas began working on a model for the memorial in 1945, only to have his initial design rejected by the New York City Art Commission, a government committee charged with reviewing public art and architecture now known as the Public Design Commission. The reasons for the rejection weren't entirely clear, but Thomas went back to work at the National Sculpture Society and replaced the white wounded soldier with a Black one. Both the Coast Guard and, eventually, the commission signed off on this change. By 1947, local and national press were reporting on a completed scale model of the Coast Guard Memorial. In an interview with the African American paper the *Pittsburgh Courier*, Thomas cited his Black crewmates as an inspiration: "They were the best gunners on the Callaway. You didn't know how important they were until the Japanese planes came over. Then all hell broke loose." He added, "It is not generally known that our service is considered the most democratic with regard to the relationship between colored and white personnel."[83] It's worth noting that one of the Coast Guard public relations officers pitching the memorial story to the *Courier* and other papers was Chief Petty Officer Alex Haley. Photos from the period show the future author of *The Autobiography of Malcolm X* and *Roots* visiting Thomas in his studio.

The *Courier* was especially interested in Thomas's memorial because it had advocated for Black representation in the armed forces from the outset of the war in 1941, when there were just four thousand Black Americans in the military and only twelve were officers. Beginning in 1942, the paper launched the Double V Campaign to remind Black Americans that they were fighting for victory over fascist enemies abroad and white supremacists at home. For the *Courier*, the war represented a singular opportunity "to persuade, embarrass, compel and shame our government and our nation...into a more enlightened attitude toward a tenth of its people!"[84] One measure of the success of the campaign was the presence by the end of the war in 1945 of over one million Black men serving in all branches of the service and thousands of Black women in the reserves.[85] Over five thousand Black men were serving in the Coast Guard in 1945.

Norman Thomas's integrated Coast Guard Memorial symbolized the kind of progress the Double V movement was hoping to see. The paper described the wounded soldier in the statue as "the first colored American to be immortalized in a national war memorial." There had been other war monuments featuring Black soldiers, like the Shaw Memorial in Boston and the Hayward Memorial in the Harlem Armory, but they were locally organized and funded. Thomas explained to the *Courier* why he took the unusual step of including the Black soldier in the sculpture:

> *From the beginning I had the idea of including a negro, I served with them, I saw them in action. I simply thought it was about time they were honored symbolically for their services to our country in every war. The Coast Guard authorities agreed.*[86]

Not long after the *Courier* interview, in the spring of 1947, Thomas finished his work on the memorial, and it was cast in bronze. Due to delays in the construction of the Battery Tunnel and the renovation of Battery Park, the sculpture would sit in storage for the next eight years.

The long-awaited unveiling of the Coast Guard Memorial came on Memorial Day 1955. Over five hundred men and women, including dignitaries from the armed forces, the government and the clergy, gathered in Battery Park, a stone's throw from New York City's bustling harbor.[87] Both local and the national press were there, and the city's public radio station, WNYC, carried special live coverage beginning with the singing of the national anthem and followed by a series of speeches, many of which were, fittingly, punctuated by horn blasts from passing ships.

Remarkably, in all the speeches, there was not a single mention of the Black soldier in the memorial. "The nine-foot memorial depicts a wounded soldier being evacuated by two armed Coast Guardsmen," was how the *New York Times* described it. But neither the *Times* nor any other papers mentioned the race of the wounded soldier.[88] And none of the Coast Guard public relations materials touched on race. What did Norman Thomas think? He was there for the dedication but made no speech and wasn't quoted in the press.

Coast Guard Memorial unveiling, Memorial Day 1955. *Coast Guard Historian.*

It's difficult to know exactly why the race of the wounded soldier was dropped from the record in 1955. *Ebony Magazine* had recently run a flattering piece on the Coast Guard, in 1952, with the subtitle "negroes fully integrated segment of sea-going service." The Coast Guard did not seem to be shy about integration. Was the silence about their interracial monument just a shocking oversight? Did the fact that Alex Haley had transferred to San Francisco in 1954, a year before the dedication, contribute? He was most likely the only Black man in the New York Public Information Office. Perhaps this also explains why there was no coverage of the dedication in the *Pittsburgh Courier* or any Black press? Norman Thomas might have answered some of these questions, but he died in 1987 at age seventy in Cuernavaca, Mexico, without shedding light on the mystery.

It wasn't until 2001 that the New York City Department of Parks and Recreation began to officially describe the monument as "interracial" on a historical sign at the site. After this official recognition of the wounded Black soldier, some critics pointed to the fact that he was shirtless and bowed and supported by clothed, upright white men as evidence that Thomas's work upheld the traditional racial hierarchy of the time.[89] Visitors can decide for themselves if they agree.

Following a redesign of Battery Park in 2021, the Coast Guard Memorial was moved to its present location just outside the Coast Guard Battery Building. At the rededication, Admiral Karl L. Schultz, commandant of the Coast Guard, spoke to the gathered crowd of guardians, including several officers of color, about African Americans who had served in the Coast Guard, like Jacob Lawrence and Alex Haley. The commandant also quoted the *Pittsburgh Courier*'s 1947 interview with Thomas, leaving no doubt about the artist's intentions to honor Black servicemen "symbolically." And just like that, the interracial nature of both the force and the monument was celebrated, not ignored.[90]

Chapter 15

GEORGE WASHINGTON CARVER AS A BOY STATUE

Young George Washington Carver by Robert Amendola, 1955. *David Jacobs.*

SCULPTOR: Robert Amendola
DEDICATED: 1955
LOCATION: George Washington Carver Houses, East 100th Street between Park and Madison
MATERIALS: Bronze
DONOR: New York City Housing Authority

INSCRIPTION:

> *George Washington Carver as a Boy. "You shall know science and science shall make you free."*
>
> *George Washington Carver, 1864–1943. Born of slave parentage in Missouri, Dr. Carver worked his way through school and then devoted his life to agricultural research for the betterment of the South and the nation. In 1923, he was awarded the Spingarn Medal "for discoveries that changed the economic life of the South" and in 1939, the Roosevelt Medal "for distinguished service in the field of science."*

If George Washington Carver is remembered for anything today, it is for inventing peanut butter, something he did not, in fact, do. He did, however, come up with over three hundred uses for the peanut and left a lasting impact on American agriculture. Born into slavery, Carver was a gifted botanist and became the first Black American to earn a bachelor of science when he graduated from Iowa State in 1894. After he earned his master's in agriculture, Booker T. Washington recruited him in 1896 to start an agricultural school at the Tuskegee Institute in Alabama. At the time, the state's main crop was cotton, and most of the rural Black population subsisted on fat bacon and corn bread. Carver made it his mission to help these sharecroppers and tenant farmers expand their diets with vegetables and become healthier and more self-sufficient. He not only taught people how to grow tomatoes but also showed them 105 ways to prepare them for eating.

Carver also innovated in soil management in the South, rotating nitrogen-fixing plants like sweet potatoes, soybeans and peanuts into cotton fields exhausted of nutrients.[91] The rotation not only increased cotton yields but also provided new sources of nutrition and alternative cash crops. Carver shared his farming advice in agriculture bulletins, which were widely read, and his achievements eventually drew the attention of Presidents from Teddy to Franklin Roosevelt, who sought Carver's agricultural advice, and Mahatma Gandhi, who consulted him on how to improve nutrition in India.

For a man who lived his life in the segregated South, Carver was conspicuously apolitical. He emphasized self-sufficiency and wrote of Black Americans, "We must get hold of the soil and work ourselves into an indispensable part and parcel of this great body politic. At the present time we are too parasitic."[92] Instead of confronting racism in the South, Carver avoided making public statements about segregation. For this reason,

Above: George Washington Carver in a field, 1906. *Library of Congress.*

Opposite: Sculptor Robert Amendola in an undated family photograph. *Amendola family.*

perhaps unfairly, he is lumped in by some with accommodationists like Booker T. Washington.

Still, Carver spent his life in Alabama working to uplift Black people, and for as much time as he devoted to developing commercial applications for crops, he never sought financial gain, famously refusing an opportunity to work for Thomas Edison.[93] Following Carver's death in 1943, FDR

created a national monument to him in Diamond, Missouri, where he grew up. This was the first national monument dedicated to a Black person, and at the time, only George Washington and Abraham Lincoln had been so honored. In the years that followed, cities and states around the country renamed schools after the great scientist.

New York City first honored Carver in 1943 with a school for adult education in Harlem and did so again in 1955, when the New York City Housing Authority (NYCHA) named a housing project for lower income residents, Carver Houses, in East Harlem after him. NYCHA then chose the sculptor Robert Amendola to make a statue of the great man to grace its southernmost courtyard just above Ninety-Ninth Street.

Robert Amendola was a very talented man. His 1996 *New York Times* obituary had the unusual headline, "Instructor to Blind and a Sculptor."[94] After graduating from Yale with a fine arts degree in 1933, he won the prestigious Prix de Rome and earned a master's as a Fellow of the American Academy in Rome in 1935. During World War II, Amendola worked as an engineering illustrator and was part of the team that designed the Corsair fighter plane, used extensively by the U.S. Navy in the Pacific Theater. Before the end of the war, he put his spatial awareness to work showing blinded veterans how to use sound to navigate their environment.[95] In addition to working with the blind for much of his life, he maintained an active sculpting career and was known for his *Stations of the Ways of the Cross* at Yale's St. Thomas More Chapel.[96]

Amendola's initial concept for the Carver sculpture was of a very large peanut with Carver's various inventions pouring out of it, but he scrapped that idea after glancing out his studio window and seeing a young boy sitting on a stone wall "engrossed in thought." Inspired, he decided to make a sculpture of Carver as a young boy instead. After a visit to Diamond, Missouri, to get a feel for Carter's childhood, he developed a charming scene: a young Carver perched dreamily on a rock, his eyes toward the sky. Amendola wrote that he drew on Carver's belief that God "made all things in nature for the good of mankind but…left to man the challenging tasks of discovering the potential and appropriate use of each." The artist imagined the budding scientist as a boy on one of his daily nature walks, scrambling up "a 10 foot pinnacle of deeply eroded ledge-rock" to balance at the top and watch a family of lizards basking in the sun. A strange plant catches his eye, and he loosens it to look more closely. "Finally he turns his face toward heaven and his heart to the plants' creator in wonder and thanksgiving." For Amendola, the plant in young Carter's hand was a symbol of his "multipetalled genius growing and flowering among adverse conditions where it seemed nothing could ever take root."[97]

Given the theme of the work, it is perhaps a bit odd to see it surrounded by apartment buildings in a sprawling metropolis, so it seems fitting that the National Park Service bought a copy of Amendola's statue in 1961 and put it in a more natural setting at the Carver National Monument, where it remains a popular attraction.

Chapter 16

DR. MARTIN LUTHER KING JR. MEMORIAL

Martin Luther King Memorial, Stan Sawyer, 1970. *David Jacobs.*

Sculptor: Stan Sawyer (1925–2014)
Dedicated: April 4, 1970
Location: Esplanade Gardens Apartments, 2569 7th Avenue, Harlem
Materials: Bronze and granite
Donor: Multiple contributors

Inscription:

I say to you today, my friends, that in spite of the difficulties and frustrations of the moment I still have a dream. It is a dream rooted in the American dream.

I have a dream that one day this nation will rise up and live out the true meaning of its creed: "We hold these truths to be self-evident; that all men are created equal."

I have a dream that one day on the red hills of Georgia the sons of former slaves and the sons of former slave owners will be able to sit down together at the table of brotherhood.

When we let freedom ring, when we let it ring from every village and every hamlet, from every state and every city, we will be able to speed up the day when all of God's children, black men and white men, Jews and Gentiles, Protestants and Catholics, will be able to join hands and sing in the words of the old Negro spiritual: "Free at last! Free at last! Thank God Almighty, we are free at last!"

"I HAVE A DREAM TODAY"
REV. DR. MARTIN LUTHER KING, JR.
January 15, 1929–April 4, 1968

In 1968, Eula Andrews of Harlem's Esplanade Gardens Apartments set out to build a statue. She was one of many Americans struggling to respond to the murder of Martin Luther King in April that year. Andrews, a member of the National Council of Negro Women, told *Jet Magazine*, "We have a dream that one day soon we hope, our people, both black and white, will be able to view the statue of the black Moses of our time." *Jet* identified Andrews as the "chairman" of a group of women who made up the King Memorial Statue Fund; their goal was to make "a living memorial to Dr. King…a stone of faith standing up for freedom."[98]

With contributions from the archbishop of New York, Terence Cardinal Cook, and local businesses like Mays department store and Woolworths, Andrews' dream became a reality. On April 4, 1970, two years after Dr. King's death, an elaborate "service of dedication" was held for what the program described as "the commemorative heroic bust in memory of Dr. Martin Luther King Jr."[99] After a prayer from

Opposite: Martin Luther King memorial button, 1968. *New York Public Library.*

Above: Sculptor Stan Sawyer in an undated CBS Radio publicity photo. *Public domain.*

Reverend Dr. George MacMurray of Mother Zion AME Church and a scripture reading from Rabbi Avraham Soltes of the American Jewish Committee, the official chorus of the 1963 March on Washington, the Eva Jessye Choir, sang "Death Ain't You Got No Shame."

While no record of the speeches from the dedication remains, the speaker lineup was an impressive who's who of Black power brokers in New York City: Percy Sutton, Tuskegee Airman, Freedom Rider, onetime lawyer to

Malcolm X and the first Black borough president of Manhattan; Charles Rangel, Korean War veteran, state assemblyman, and future New York City congressman; and Eleanor Holmes Norton, head of Mayor John Lindsay's Commission for Human Rights. Norton, a graduate of Yale Law School, cut her teeth as an organizer for the Student Non-Violent Coordinating Committee in Mississippi and has been an outspoken advocate for women's rights and Black rights as the congresswoman representing the District of Columbia since 1991. The strength of the dedication lineup was a measure of not only the importance of King's life but also the influence of Eula Andrews and her committee of determined women.

Among the crowd at the unveiling was the sculptor, Stan Sawyer. It's not clear how Andrews and her committee from Esplanade Gardens found Sawyer, but it's possible he was recommended by the staff at New York's Sculpture House, where much of his work, including the King bust, was cast. Sawyer, a veteran of World War II, was a pioneering television host in the 1950s on the children's show *Captain Jet*. He also worked in radio and was known in Boston as the Man of a Thousand Voices. Sawyer also made a name for himself announcing commercials for Nathan's Hot Dogs, Burlington Coat Factory, Maxwell House Coffee and many others. Sawyer's work as a freelance announcer took very little time—so little, in fact, that he claimed he "never worked more than 50 hours a year." And he put this free time to good use, developing his sculpting skills, something he had played around with since childhood.[100]

Before the King commission, Sawyer was known for his busts of comedians George Burns and Jerry Lewis as well as political figures like Eleanor Roosevelt, John F. Kennedy and Robert Kennedy. Sawyer claimed he felt a personal connection to King, whom, like Andrews, he described as the "African American Moses." He decided to sculpt a bust of King in the wake of his assassination. "It affected me emotionally," Sawyer said. "He was a leader who had a vision."[101] Sawyer's interest in King as a subject persisted, and years later, in 1991, he was commissioned to make a different bust of the fallen civil rights leader for the city of Rahway in New Jersey.

Chapter 17

GEORGE WASHINGTON CARVER MONUMENT

Bust of George Washington Carver, Richmond Barthé, 1977. *Bronx Community College Archives.*

SCULPTOR: Richmond Barthé
DEDICATED: 1977
LOCATION: Hall of Fame for Great Americans, Bronx Community College
ARCHITECT: Stanford White
MATERIALS: Bronze
DONOR: Tuskegee Institute

Inscription:

> *GEORGE WASHINGTON CARVER, 1864–1943*
>
> *OF COURSE IT HAS ALWAYS BEEN THE ONE GREAT IDEAL OF MY LIFE TO BE OF THE GREATEST GOOD TO THE GREATEST NUMBER OF "MY PEOPLE" AND TO THIS END I HAVE BEEN PREPARING MYSELF THESE MANY YEARS, FEELING AS I DO THAT THIS LINE OF EDUCATION IS THE KEY TO UNLOCKING THE GOLDEN DOOR OF FREEDOM TO OUR PEOPLE.*

On April 23, 1977, crowds gathered at the Tuskegee Institute Chapel in Alabama for the enshrinement of scientist and inventor George Washington Carver in the Hall of Fame for Great Americans. Carver was just the second Black American enshrined in the hall; the first was Booker T. Washington (see page 74). Carver's election to the hall had been a long time coming and was the result of a concerted effort by Tuskegee Institute president Luther H. Foster and president emeritus Frederick D. Patterson. The two men led a nationwide letter-writing campaign for Carver starting in 1968 when he became eligible for the hall, twenty-five years after his death. A majority vote of the hall's 134 electors was needed for selection, and while Carver fell short in the 1970 election, in 1973, he garnered 104 votes to lead a group of distinguished inductees: Justice Louis Brandeis, President Franklin D. Roosevelt and composer John Philip Sousa.[102]

The celebration for Carver took place at Tuskegee instead of at the hall in the Bronx because Carver taught there, and the institute was instrumental in getting him elected to the hall (for more on Carver, see page 90). In the keynote address, Black historian John Hope Franklin reminded his audience that as Carter came of age following Reconstruction, "the risks of bodily harm and spiritual degradation were about as great in New York and Iowa as they were in South Carolina and Alabama." Carver, Franklin continued, felt such a sense of responsibility to Black people that he sacrificed some of his own ambitions as a scientist: "If George Washington Carver had not been driven by the strongly felt need to formulate programs of scientific agriculture that would raise the living standard for black farmers in the South, he may well have been the country's leading mycologist." One of Carter's greatest contributions, said Franklin, was revolutionizing agriculture in the South at a time when it relied too heavily on monoculture, like tobacco in Virginia and the Carolinas or Cotton in the Deep South. "Carver," Franklin claimed, "was more responsible than

Daniel T. Williams (*left*), Tuskegee Institute archivist, and Elaine Thomas (*right*), curator of the Carver Museum, at the unveiling of the George Washington Carver bust at the Tuskegee Institute. 1977. *Bronx Community College Archives.*

any other single person for unlocking the shackles that bound Southerners to one-crop staple agriculture."[103]

Carver was widely recognized for his invention of over three hundred uses for the peanut, and Tuskegee had hoped to lure President Jimmy Carter to the event. Carter, famously, made a fortune from his family's peanut farm in Plains, Georgia, and that money helped drive his successful campaigns for governor of Georgia and president of the United States. Carter was unable to attend, but in a telegram from the White House to the event organizers, he acknowledged his debt to Carver: "As a Southerner whose family, like many others, benefited from Dr. Carver's brilliant and innovative research on the peanut, I have of course a personal interest in honoring his life's work."

The event made national news in both the Black and white press. Much was written about Carver's love of nature and his passion for science, but the *New York Times* chose to focus on the hall's history of exclusion:

> *More than 200 years after Crispus Attucks died in the Boston Massacre and more than 100 years after the abolitionist activism of Sojourner Truth, the Black population of the Hall of Fame for Great Americans will double today—to a total of two.*

White reporter Laurie Johnston's impatient tone reflected a relatively new attitude from the *Times*. As late as 1965, the Gray Lady had published an unabashedly positive account of one elderly southern woman's campaign to get Confederate President Jefferson Davis elected to the hall.[104] While the shift in attitude was undoubtedly influenced by the civil rights and Black Power movements, it was perhaps also spurred by growing outrage at the fact that General Robert E. Lee had been one of the original inductees in 1900 and General Stonewall Jackson was installed in 1957.[105]

The Tuskegee Institute donated funds for the Carver statue, and the Hall of Fame Art Committee chose the same Black artist who had completed a bust of Booker T. Washington thirty years earlier, Richmond Barthé (see page 74). Barthé had gone on to an international career, including major pieces of public sculpture, like *Toussaint L'Ouverture* (1952) and *Jacques Dessalines* (1954), both depicting generals in the Haitian Revolution, in Port-au-Prince. But after several years in Italy without much work, he sorely needed the $5,000 commission, and he returned to New York to take the job.[106] Barthé based the bust on a photo of a middle-aged Carver. When the finished work was installed, it brought the grand total of statues in the Hall of Fame by Black artists to a disappointing total of one.[107]

Carver's bust was the ninety-seventh to find a niche in the Bronx's Great Hall and among the last. Only Sousa and FDR came after. Since its founding at New York University's uptown campus in 1900, the hall had drawn thousands of visitors annually, but after Bronx Community College (BCC) bought the campus in 1973, the school administration chose to end elections in 1976. BCC made the decision because the site was no longer drawing tourists to its corner of a borough with a growing reputation for crime. Maintaining the outdoor site was a growing liability for the community college, and the fact that the neighborhood and student body were (and remain) mostly Black and Latino also led to ambivalent feelings about a hall mostly full of dead white men. In a 1993 interview with the *New York Times*, school president and former Tuskegee Airman Roscoe C. Brown was blunt about the hall's shortcomings:

> *In terms of who is in and who is not, I'm ashamed to be associated with it. Of the 107 people in the Hall, there are only 11 women, 2 blacks, 1 Jew and no Catholics....If it's a monument to anything, it's a monument to the sexism and racism of the elite white males who dominated in the first half of this century.*[108]

In August 2017, following the white supremacist rally in Charlottesville, Virginia, when many communities around the country raced to remove their Confederate monuments, New York Governor Andrew Cuomo called for the removal of the Lee and Jackson busts from the hall. BCC President

Thomas A. Isekenegbe obliged. "Embracing difference," Isekenegbe said in a statement, "includes creating space where all people feel respected, welcome and valued."[109] It's worth noting that, for reasons unknown, the bust of Sidney Lanier, the "poet of the Confederacy," was not removed.

While statues of great Americans are no longer being installed in the hall, Barthé's George Washington Carver bust remains in the graceful colonnade, which is open to the public and well worth the trip to University Heights in the Bronx.

Chapter 18

JACKIE ROBINSON MONUMENT

Jackie Robinson Monument, Inge Hardison, 1981.
David Jacobs.

SCULPTOR: Ruth Inge Hardison (1914–2016)
DEDICATED: November 10, 1981
LOCATION: West 147th Street and Bradhurst Avenue
ARCHITECT: Aymar Embury II
MATERIALS: Bronze
SIZE: H: 3'
DONOR: New York City Department of Cultural Affairs' Community Arts Development, funded by U.S. Department of Housing and Urban Development

Inscription:
Top plaque:

> *JACKIE ROBINSON, 1919–1972, FIRST BLACK MAJOR LEAGUE BASEBALL PLAYER. "LIFE OWES ME NOTHING. BASEBALL OWES ME NOTHING. BUT I CANNOT, AS AN INDIVIDUAL, REJOICE IN THE GOOD THINGS I HAVE BEEN PERMITTED TO WORK FOR AND LEARN WHILE THE HUMBLEST OF MY BROTHERS IS DOWN IN A DEEP HOLE HOLLERING FOR HELP AND NOT BEING HEARD."*

Bottom plaque:

> *SCULPTURE OF JACKIE ROBINSON BY INGE HARDISON, PRODUCED BY HARLEM CULTURAL COUNCIL, INC. WITH A GRANT FROM THE NEW YORK CITY DEPARTMENT OF CULTURAL AFFAIRS COMMUNITY ARTS DEVELOPMENT PROGRAM FUNDED BY THE UNITED STATES DEPARTMENT OF HOUSING AND URBAN DEVELOPMENT.*

While most know Jackie Robinson as the man who broke baseball's color barrier with the Brooklyn Dodgers in 1947, he also broke a barrier in public art when became the first real athlete of any race honored with a public statue in New York City. It happened on November 10, 1981, when his widow, Rachel, unveiled a nearly three-foot bronze portrait bust in the lobby of the recreation center in Harlem's Jackie Robinson Park.[110] In his time with the Dodgers, the future Hall of Famer was Rookie of the Year in 1947, a National League MVP in 1949 and a key member of the team that brought Brooklyn its first and only World Series title in 1955. Robinson used his notoriety to support the civil rights movement and uplift Black people by fundraising and demonstrating, often with Martin Luther King.[111] He could not, as he said, "rejoice in the good things…while the humblest of my brothers is down in a deep hole hollering for help."[112]

The dedication of the Robinson memorial was a moment years in the making, due in large part to the efforts of African American Councilman Fred Samuel of Harlem's Fifth District. Among the powers of city council members is the ability to rename parks and streets. Samuel, like Robinson, used his power to uplift and defend Black Americans.[113] In 1974, he introduced a local law to change Harlem's stretch of Seventh Avenue to Adam Clayton Powell Jr. Boulevard, after the late congressman. In 1978, he pushed through a law to suspend the licenses of taxi drivers who refused

to take fares to certain neighborhoods, like Harlem, and convinced the council to name the park across from the United Nations after the first person of African descent to win a Nobel Peace Prize, Ralph Bunche. And that same year, he got a local law passed to rename Colonial Park after Jackie Robinson, a widely admired figure in Harlem, where his son, David Robinson, was also an affordable housing organizer.[114]

With a grant from the New York City Department of Cultural Affairs' Community Arts Development to produce a statue of Robinson, the Harlem Cultural Council selected the artist Inge Hardison, a woman known for sculpting Black American heroes. Born in Portsmouth, Virginia, in 1914, the grandchild of slaves, Hardison came to Brooklyn with her family as part of the Great Migration in search of better opportunities. After graduating from Girls High School, she found steady work as a Broadway actress, playing the role of Topsy in a 1936 adaptation of *Uncle Tom's Cabin*. A versatile artist, she also took photographs and wrote poetry, including an ode to "a day for dreaming in the sun, for telling worsted tales, for languid ease," which the *New York Times* published in 1938. While modeling for classes at the Art Students League of New York, she began playing with the sculpting clay and soon found she had a talent, which she chose to develop by studying fine art at Vassar College in the '40s.[115]

In 1963, after learning that there was only one statue of a Black person, Booker T. Washington, in the Bronx Hall of Fame of Great Americans (see page 74), Hardison began a series of cast-iron busts, *Negro Giants in History*. She started with Harriet Tubman and moved on to, among others, Frederick Douglass, W.E.B. Du Bois and Sojourner Truth.[116] In the late '60s, Old Taylor, an established Kentucky straight bourbon whiskey brand, saw Hardison's statues as a marketing opportunity in the Black community. In an unusual partnership, they commissioned her to make a plaster series of great Black Americans called *Ingenious Americans*, which they advertised and sold in *Ebony* and *Jet* magazines. This series included Black men like colonial-era scientist and surveyor Benjamin Banneker, arctic explorer Matthew Henson and Dr. Drew Hansen, a pioneer in blood preservation.

The busts sold for just five dollars each because, as Hardison said in a letter to a friend, "I feel that everyone should have the pleasure of owning a

Opposite: Jackie Robinson publicity photo, 1954. *Library of Congress.*

Above: Inge Hardison, undated photo. *Wikimedia Commons.*

Right: "Old Taylor Presents: 6 Ingenious Americans" advertisement in the June 1971 issue of *Ebony Magazine*. *Public domain.*

work of art." She also believed in spreading the word about the important role of Black people in U.S. history and exhibited and sold her statues with her manager and companion, Margaret McCaden, at flea markets, schools and museums for many years. "By memorializing such great, selfless people," she once said, "I have been able to put within the experience of many schoolchildren, college students and adults those much-needed models of inspiration."[117]

In 2016, Inge Hardison died of complications from Alzheimer's at the age of 102. In addition to her sculpture of Jackie Robinson, her work remains on display at Intermediate School 74 in the Bronx, Medgar Evers College in Brooklyn and Mount Sinai Hospital in Manhattan.[118] In 2005, New York got its second statue of Jackie Robinson when the Jackie Robinson and Pee Wee Reese Monument was dedicated in Coney Island outside Maimonides Park, home of the Cyclones (see page 144).

Chapter 19

REVEREND BENJAMIN J. LOWRY MONUMENT

Reverend Benjamin James Lowry Monument, Robert W. Pugh, 1982. *David Jacobs.*

SCULPTOR: Robert W. Pugh
DEDICATED: July 31, 1982
LOCATION: Underhill, Pacific, Washington and Atlantic Avenues, Brooklyn
MATERIALS: Stainless steel, ebony mist granite
SIZE: Bust H × W × D: 2'2" × 1'6"× 11"
Pedestal H × W × D: 6'7" × 2'6" × 2'6"
DONOR: Zion Baptist Church and community

Inscription:

> *REV. BENJAMIN J. LOWRY*

Proper left side:

> *REV. BENJAMIN J. LOWRY. "LIFE HAS TAUGHT ME THAT THERE IS NO SUBSTITUTE FOR PERSISTENCE AND HARD WORK. NO MATTER HOW GIFTED OR TALENTED AN INDIVIDUAL, LIFE DOES NOT GUARANTEE HIM SUCCESS. SUCCESSFUL AND WORTHWHILE LIVES COME FROM CONSECRATION, DEDICATION, PERSISTENCE AND FAITH IN GOD." —DR. B.J. LOWRY*

Back:

> *REV. BENJAMIN J. LOWRY. DEDICATED JULY 31, 1982.*

Proper right side:

> *REV. BENJAMIN J. LOWRY, D.D. PH.D LL.D, UNIVERSALIST SCHOLAR DEDICATED TO RELIGIOUS SERVICE. HIS INNER STRENGTH AND MANIFEST PRACTICE OF THE SPIRITUAL VALUES HE TEACHES WILL ALWAYS BE A VITAL FORCE AMONG US. —ZION BAPTIST CHURCH INC. AND THE COMMUNITY*

On July 31, 1982, the aged Reverend Benjamin J. Lowry, along with Mayor Ed Koch and other dignitaries, gathered in Brooklyn for an unusual ceremony. In it, the ninety-two year-old Lowry became the first living New Yorker to attend the unveiling of a public statue dedicated in his honor. The shiny, stainless steel bust of the elderly Lowry with his eyes lifted to the sky was by Robert Pugh, the African American owner of the Keystone Monument Company in Brooklyn. Pugh's business was funerary monuments, but he was also known for an engraved monolith of Frederick Johnson, Althea Gibson's first tennis coach, in a park dedicated to him in Harlem. (See page 163 for more on Althea Gibson).[119]

Lowry had served Brooklyn's Zion Baptist Church since 1921, and in 1973, according to church records, he became the first pastor in New York City to lead his church in observance of Martin Luther King's birthday.[120] In 1981, over three thousand attended special services for King at Zion Baptist, while

Reverend B.J. Lowry (*seated, left*) at monument dedication, with Mayor Ed Koch (center) and Brooklyn borough president Howard Golden (*right*). *NYC Parks/Art and Antiquities.*

churches, schools and the streets of New York rang with remembrances of the slain civil rights leader—all part of a movement that would make Martin Luther King Day a national holiday in 1986.[121]

The details of Reverend Lowry's early life are unclear, but the rough sketch reveals the arc of a striver. He was born in 1891 and, according to his grandson, A. Leon Lowry II, grew up on the Lowry Plantation in Louisville, Georgia, where his parents had once been enslaved. When his father died and his mother remarried, Lowry found his stepfather too strict for his liking. He began saving his money, and at the age of fourteen or fifteen, he left home for Savannah, where he met and eventually married Evelyn Soloman. In the early years of the Great Migration, the couple made their way north to Connecticut, where Lowry worked on a tobacco farm while finishing high school. A keen student, he earned admission to Virginia Seminary and College in Lynchburg, Virginia, a historically black college, where he earned a divinity degree. After graduating, Lowry moved with Evelyn to New York City, where he found work as a postman in Brooklyn. As it happened, Zion

Baptist Church at 523 Washington Avenue in Clinton Hill was on Lowry's route—and in need of a pastor.[122] Lowry began attending services, and in 1921, he became Zion Baptist's pastor, a position he would hold until his death, sixty-three years later, in 1985. One of his sons, Alfonso Leon Lowry, followed him into the ministry and was known for teaching Dr. Martin Luther King theology at Morehouse.[123]

Tall and elegantly dressed, with a clear voice, Reverend Lowry helped organize protests against discrimination and the lack of construction jobs for Blacks and Latinos during the civil rights era. Along with other clergymen, he met with and extracted a promise from Governor Nelson Rockefeller to enforce antidiscrimination laws, find pathways for minorities into union membership and withhold funding from construction projects where discrimination was proven to have occurred.[124]

In 1964, David Halberstam of the *New York Times* (perhaps best known for his Vietnam reporting) wrote that Reverend Lowry, then chairman of the Ministers Group of Brooklyn and Long Island, had announced the group's support of Hasidic Jews in Crown Heights in fighting crime. Rabbi Samuel Schrage of the United Lubavitcher Yeshivoth formed the neighborhood patrols known as the Maccabees (after the Jewish warriors) in response to a rash of "muggings and acts of violence," by which "Jews felt they were being terrorized and harassed." Despite initial concerns about vigilantism, African Americans in the Bedford Stuyvesant area agreed to ride along on the Hasidic patrols, which alerted police to potential crime and sometimes intervened to help victims. The partnership was so successful in reducing crime that it was eventually disbanded.[125]

During Lowry's long tenure at Zion Baptist, he performed a remarkable 1,977 marriages, 3,569 baptisms and 1,039 eulogies.[126] It was for this extraordinary service that the congregation wanted to honor their pastor with a monument. In 1980, the officers of the church reached out to Mary Pinkett, New York's first Black councilwoman, with a proposal to place the statue in a small, derelict park near Zion Baptist's Washington Avenue location. Pinkett supported the plan by introducing a local law to rename the park Lowry Triangle and also helped shepherd the monument through the Parks Department and community board approval process.[127] Pinkett, who represented Brooklyn on the city council for thirty years, later introduced a local law to rename a park in Prospect Heights after the astronaut Dr. Ronald McNair (see page 113).[128]

Chapter 20

DR. RONALD E. McNAIR MONUMENT

Dr. Ronald E. McNair Monument, Ogundipe Fayomi, 1994. *David Jacobs.*

SCULPTOR: Ogundipe Fayomi (a.k.a. Claude Audrey)
DEDICATED: June 14, 1994
LOCATION: Dr. Ronald E. McNair Park, Eastern Parkway, Washington to Classon Avenues
MEDIUM: Bust: bronze
Obelisk: red granite
SIZE: Obelisk H × W: 9' × 5'6" at base
DONOR: Percent for Art, New York City

Inscription:
Center:

DEDICATED TO THE MEMORY OF DR. RONALD MCNAIR, BORN OCTOBER 21, 1950, LAKE CITY, SOUTH CAROLINA, DIED JANUARY 28, 1986, ABOARD THE SPACE SHUTTLE CHALLENGER, PHYSICIST, ASTRONAUT, TEACHER, MUSICIAN, ATHLETE. "MY WISH IS THAT WE WOULD ALLOW THIS PLANET TO BE THE BEAUTIFUL OASIS THAT SHE IS, AND ALLOW OURSELVES TO LIVE MORE IN THE PEACE THAT SHE GENERATES."

Proper left:

"TRULY THERE IS NO MORE BEAUTIFUL SIGHT THAN TO SEE THE EARTH FROM A SPACE BEYOND."

Proper right:

"THE SATISFYING THING ABOUT PHYSICS ITSELF IS THE FEELING OF HAVING UNDERSTOOD AND UNLOCKED SOMETHING HERETOFORE UNKNOWN." "DEFY AND SIMPLY IGNORE ANY OF THE INEVITABLE OBSTACLES THAT WILL IMPEDE THE PURSUIT OF YOUR GOAL."

On proper right plaque:

SCULPTOR OGUNDIPE FAYOMI. DR. RONALD MCNAIR MONUMENT. MATERIAL: BRONZE & GRANITE. COLLECTION OF THE CITY OF NEW YORK. COMMISSIONED BY DEPARTMENT OF CULTURAL AFFAIRS PERCENT FOR ART PROGRAMS. SPONSORED BY DEPARTMENT OF PARKS & RECREATION. ACCESSION NUMBER: PFA 94.1.

In 1950, the odds of a poor Black child born in a small town in the segregated South going to space were long, but by all measures, Ronald Erwin McNair was truly exceptional. In addition to earning a PhD in physics from MIT, he was a fifth-degree black belt in karate and an accomplished saxophone player. And after gaining a national reputation for his work on laser physics at the Hughes Laboratory, McNair was selected in 1978 by NASA for the space program along with two other Black candidates, Guion Bluford and Frederick Gregory. In 1984, he became the second Black man in space (Bluford was the first) when he flew as a mission specialist on the fourth flight of the shuttle *Challenger*. During the flight, he operated the shuttle's robotic arm and, in another first, played the saxophone in orbit. One can only imagine what other extraordinary feats he might have achieved had his life not been tragically cut short seventy-three seconds into the doomed final mission of the *Challenger* on January 28, 1986. McNair left behind a wife and two children.[129]

Two years before his death, in a 1984 commencement address at the University of South Carolina, McNair described a pivotal moment in his life. As a freshman at North Carolina A&T, he was determined to become a physics major until he met some other prospective physics majors who seemed to know a lot more about the subject then he did. "The only physics that I knew anything about," he said, "was a theory of propagation of tobacco leaves"—a reference to a childhood spent picking tobacco leaves. Doubting himself, McNair turned briefly to the Music Department. But thinking he hadn't given physics a real try, he met with a guidance counselor, who gave him a battery of standardized tests over the course of three days. As McNair described it, after examining the results, "she kind of shook her head, looked back up at me, and she said, 'I think you ought to go ahead and try physics, because I think you're good enough.' That's all I needed." Buoyed by words of encouragement at a critical moment, McNair went on to complete his doctorate in physics at MIT.[130]

In the wake of McNair's death, towns and cities across the country rushed to rename schools, parks and libraries in his honor. Greensboro dedicated a bust of the late astronaut at his alma mater, North Carolina A&T, and New Orleans even renamed Robert E. Lee Elementary after him.[131] New York City would eventually name an elementary and a middle school in his honor. And less than a year later, Councilwoman Mary Pinkett of Brooklyn, the first Black woman elected to the city council, successfully introduced legislation to rename Prospect Heights' Guider Park, next to the Brooklyn Museum, Dr. Ronald E. McNair Park.[132]

During a renovation in 1994, funds were set aside for a memorial to McNair under the Percent for Art Program (PFA), which required that 1 percent of the budget for city-funded projects be spent on art in public facilities like municipal buildings, schools and parks. The McNair memorial was chosen by PFA not just because of his achievements but also because of his race. In an email, Jennifer McGregor, who was a director of the program in the early '90s, recalled the significance of the McNair memorial: "The lack of statues or tributes to African Americans was keenly acknowledged, and this presented an important opportunity for recognition."[133]

Unveiling of Dr. Ronald E. McNair Monument, June 14, 1994. *NYC Parks/Art and Antiquities.*

Since its inception in 1983, PFA, administered by the New York City Department of Cultural Affairs, has provided over $41 million for nearly three hundred completed projects. To make up for a general failure to include minority artists in past city projects, PFA made a concerted effort to commission, as it says on its website, "artists of all races and backgrounds that reflect the diversity of New York City."[134] For example, out of roughly five hundred applicants for the Ronald McNair Memorial project, PFA chose the Black artist and designer Ogundipe Fayomi. Fayomi, a graduate of Pratt Institute in 1973 with a BFA in sculpture, lived in Crown Heights near the memorial site and was—and remains—committed to creating positive images of African Americans.

In 2008, in an interview with LaVerne Cody Gittens on her Manhattan Neighborhood Network show *LINKLaV*, Fayomi described how disappointed he was to learn that out of the roughly two thousand public statues in the Parks Department throughout the five boroughs, only "twelve or so" were of people of color. "If we are talking about educating our children," he said, "and giving positive and strong images to uplift young people and the consciousness of Black people, we have to have our images in all our parks in our communities."[135]

In June 1994, McNair's family and friends, including his second grade teacher and his NASA colleagues, gathered in McNair park to dedicate his memorial. The sculpture, a bronze bust of McNair in NASA garb, is recessed in a red granite pyramid-like obelisk. In a conversation with the author, Fayomi said his intent was to create the impression of McNair as a passenger on a ship heading to space.[136] Bronze plaques with scenes from the astronaut's life flank the bust, and etched on all sides of the obelisk are quotes by McNair. Like many astronauts, McNair was profoundly moved after seeing Earth from space during his first mission on *Challenger*. "My wish," he said, "is that we would all allow this planet to be the beautiful oasis that she is, and allow ourselves to live more in the peace that she generates."[137]

Chapter 21

PETER AND WILLIE STATUE

Peter and Willie, Otto Neals, 1997. *David Jacobs.*

SCULPTOR: Otto Neals (1931–)
DEDICATED: June 20, 1997
LOCATION: Imagination Playground, Ocean Avenue and Lincoln Road
ARCHITECT: Christian Zimmerman
MATERIALS: Figures: bronze
Boulder: basalt
SIZE: Boulder approx. W × D: 9' × 4'
DONOR: Ezra Jack Keats Foundation (sculpture only), New York City Parks Department (boulder)

Inscription:

Peter & Willie. From the books by Ezra Jack Keats. Otto Neals, sculptor. Gift of Ezra Jack Keats Foundation. © OTTO NEALS, 1997.

The small children's playground in Brooklyn's Prospect Park near the intersection of Ocean Avenue and Lincoln Road is unlike most. You won't see children going their highest on swings or their fastest down slides. Instead, it's called the Imagination Playground, and there, children are encouraged to push their minds to new heights of fancy with a gentle nudge from a fountain shaped like a dragon, a small stage and a bronze statue of a Black child reading on a large rock, extending a hand to pet his dog. A small, empty bronze chair sits invitingly before the scene.

The boy, Peter, and the dog, Willie, are featured characters in a series of children's books. The story of how they came to be memorialized involves two artists.[138]

The first artist was Jacob Ezra Katz. Born in 1916 into a poor family of Polish Jews in East New York, Brooklyn, Katz distinguished himself as an artist from an early age. In high school, he won a national Scholastic Award for a painting of homeless men warming themselves around a fire. During World War II, he joined the army, where his talents were put to use developing designs for camouflage. After the war, he changed his name to the less Jewish-sounding Keats, thinking this would make it easier to find work as a commercial artist. He'd faced antisemitism in the army and throughout his life. This discrimination made him sympathetic to others with similar experiences and was part of the inspiration behind his breakthrough children's book *The Snowy Day*.[139]

The illustrations in *The Snowy Day*, winner of a Caldecott Medal in 1963, create the magical world of a child through a delightful combination of collage, handmade stamps and ink.[140] It's a fairly typical children's story about a boy, Peter, going out to play in the snow—except the boy is Black, a rarity at the time. Keats later explained the significance of this choice: "None of the manuscripts I'd been illustrating featured any black kids—except for token blacks in the background. My book would have him there simply because he should have been there all along."[141]

After breaking the color barrier in children's publishing, Keats continued with a series of books following Peter as he grew up in Brooklyn with his friends, family and faithful dachshund, Willie. Throughout his remarkable career, Keats wrote and illustrated twenty-two books for children and illustrated an

Above: Author and artist Ezra Jack Keats in the 1980s. *Ezra Jack Keats Foundation.*

Opposite: Cover of *The Snowy Day*, by Ezra Jack Keats. *Ezra Jack Keats Foundation.*

additional eighty-five. In 1964, he launched the Ezra Jack Keats Foundation to support arts and literacy and traveled the country, visiting schools and encouraging young children to read, until his death in 1983. *The Snowy Day* remains the most checked out book in the New York Public Library (ahead of *The Cat in the Hat*), with 485,583 checkouts and counting.[142]

In 1990, after sponsoring an outdoor storytelling series for children at different locations in Prospect Park for a number of years, Keats Foundation leaders Lillie and Martin Pope approached the Prospect Park Alliance with the idea of creating a permanent location for readings, similar to José de Creeft's *Alice in Wonderland* in Central Park. The Popes wanted the statue to be of Peter from *The Snowy Day* because, like the children who played in the park, he was from Brooklyn. The Alliance, led by Tupper Thomas, agreed, offering to make a home for the statue in an Ocean Avenue playground that was in need of renovation.

The project went forward with help from Black Councilwoman Una Clark, who provided funds for the playground from her budget. Funding for the statue came from the Keats Foundation, Harper Collins Children's Books,

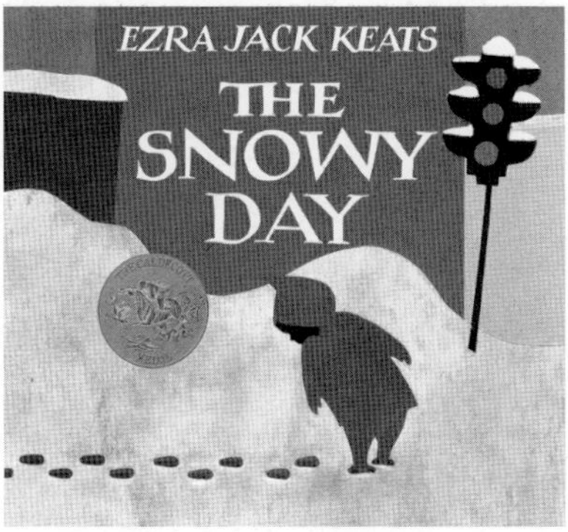

Viking Books and Morton Schindel, a producer who turned children's books, including *The Snowy Day*, into animated films. The Prospect Park Alliance and the Keats Foundation put out a call for proposals and worked with the Municipal Art Commission (now the Public Design Commission) to identify a Black sculptor for the job.[143] The Black artist Otto Neals's submission, which combined elements of Keats's works *Whistle for Willie* and *Peter's Chair*, was the winner.[144]

Otto Neals was born in Lake City, South Carolina, in 1931, and his family moved to Brooklyn when he was just four. From an early age, he loved drawing, and he studied commercial art at the High School of Specialty Trades (now known as Westinghouse). After graduating, he served in the army for two years, returning home to work for the U.S. Postal Service. There, Neals applied for positions in the art department, but because he was Black, he was denied for seven years, until the Black postal union intervened, securing him a position in the art department. Eventually, Neals became the head illustrator for the Staten Island, Brooklyn and Long Island City branches, and in 1976, he was commissioned to make a sculpture of the thirteen-cent stamps celebrating the U.S. Bicentennial based on Archibald Willard's painting *The Spirit of '76*. The four-by-eight-foot bas-relief wood carving Neals created greeted customers at Brooklyn's Cadman Plaza post office for many years. In the late '80s, after almost four decades on the job, Neals retired from the post office and focused solely on his art.[145]

A mostly self-taught artist with a deep interest in his African heritage, Neals frequently traveled to the Caribbean and Africa. "My talent as an artist," Neals wrote on his website, "comes directly from my ancestors." Neals developed his Afrocentric vision in the 1960s and '70s as a member of the Weusi Arts Collective. *Weusi* means "blackness" in Swahili, and the collective was part of the Black Arts Movement, which saw art as a key to Black liberation. "I try to paint and sculpt African people," Neals wrote, "working always to portray those characteristics true of their beauty, their power and their love." Today, his work can be found in the National Museum of Ghana, the Studio Museum in Harlem and the Schomburg Center for Research in Black Culture.[146]

Artist Otto Neals and "Peter," 1997. *Paul Martinka.*

Peter and Willie was the first major public commission of Otto Neals's career, but his background seemed to make him an obvious choice to bring Keats's work to life. At the unveiling in Imagination Playground on June 21, 1997, the sixty-five-year-old Neals told a crowd of adults and children that the park was a place for "our young people to use their imaginations, to use their talents."[147]

Both Neals and the playground's designer, Christian Zimmerman of the Prospect Park Alliance, received the New York Art Commission Excellence in Design Award for their work. Another measure of Neals's success can be found on the statue of Peter itself. The blue patina coating the bronze, which tends to wear away over time, has worn away from his ears first. The children, it seems, are so enchanted by Neals's work that they whisper their secrets to Peter.[148]

Chapter 22

DUKE ELLINGTON MEMORIAL

Duke Ellington Memorial, Robert Graham, 1997. *David Jacobs.*

SCULPTOR: Robert Graham (1938–2008)
DEDICATED: July 1, 1997
LOCATION: Duke Ellington Circle, 110th Street and 5th Avenue
MATERIALS: Bronze, red granite, aggregate
SIZE: Ellington figure H: 8'
Each caryatid H: 4'
Each triform column H: 10'
Sculpture total H: 25'; upper plaque H × W: 5" × 10"; lower plaque H × W: 2¼" × 7½"
DONOR: Duke Ellington Memorial Fund

Inscription:

> *Edward Kennedy "Duke" Ellington, 1899–1974, orchestra leader, pianist, composer.*
>
> *A gift to the City of New York from Bobby Short, founder, the Duke Ellington Memorial Fund and thousands of Ellington fans around the world. Dedicated July 1, 1997.*

In the summer of 1979, while walking in the Jardin du Monastère de Cimiez, a formal garden in Nice, the singer and pianist Bobby Short came across something he could not find in his hometown of New York: a bronze monument to a Black American jazz musician. This encounter, with a bust of Louis Armstrong, caused Short to marvel, as he told the *New York Times* in 1997: "How strange that here, in France, they have found time and space for a tribute to a black American jazz musician, but in New York I could think of nothing like that."

How strange indeed. Fortunately for Short, his long residence at the Upper East Side's Café Carlyle had made him a beloved star with lots of wealthy connections. According to the *Times*, he formed the Duke Ellington Memorial Fund and raised over $1 million with events "in the Rainbow Room, at Lincoln Center and here and there around town" to pay for a monument to the richly deserving Ellington.[149] Little did Short know that the memorial would take nearly two decades to erect and cause no small amount of controversy.

Short's fundraising success was made possible in part because Ellington was one of the most popular musical talents of the twentieth century. Elegant and ambitious, Ellington blazed a trail for jazz in the 1920s and '30s leading, a big band of virtuoso performers during long-term residencies at the Cotton Club and two tours in Europe. Born in 1899, Edward "Duke" Kennedy Ellington was a gifted pianist and composer from an early age. Along with greats like Louis Armstrong and Ella Fitzgerald, he was a star of the swing era and featured regularly on the radio and in films.[150]

In 1941, to celebrate the opening of New York's newest subway line, connecting Harlem to lower Manhattan, Tempo Music, the label Ellington founded, released "Take the A Train," a chart-topping success for which he is arguably best known.[151] When he died in 1974 of complications from lung cancer, over twelve thousand people attended his funeral at St. John the Divine in Morningside Heights. Music critic Ralph J. Gleason, reached for comment after Ellington's death, marveled at his talent: "He's the greatest musician America's ever produced. America's greatest composer of any kind of music."[152]

How do you honor such a legend? And in a prime location like Central Park, no less? The man chosen for the job by Bobby Short's memorial committee was the Los Angeles–based Mexican sculptor Robert Graham. Graham was known for a number of monumental pieces, including *Olympic Gateway*: striking, headless, male and female nudes at the entrance to the Los Angeles Memorial Coliseum for the 1984 Olympics and a massive bronze fist in Detroit in honor of heavyweight boxing champion Joe Louis. While Short initially imagined a simple bust of Ellington, Graham convinced him otherwise. "He felt it should be something grand and elegant," said Short, "the way he perceived Duke Ellington to be." Graham's vision for the memorial has an eight-foot-tall Ellington statue on a platform ten feet above the street standing beside a piano.[153] Three pillars support the platform, each topped by three Black female nudes—and herein lies a problem.

The use of women as architectural support in this way has its roots in Greek classical architecture: the caryatids of the Erechtheion just a stone's throw from the Parthenon are a sterling example. Still, some felt, and many continue to feel, that the image of a man supported by nine naked women sent the wrong message. In 1990, when the first photos of the work in progress were released, the *New York Times* took the temperature of residents around the future Central Park location. Jaribu Hill, forty-one, from a local youth leadership program, seemed to capture the essence of the issue: "I think it represents something that I hope they don't mean, but they probably do mean—some kind of male domination. And if they don't believe that, they are not sensitive."[154] Graham argued that the women represented muses, Greek goddesses of inspiration. "I don't know what the issue is," he said. "There's nudity all over the place. The idea of muses, of things springing from their heads, it's a very classical idea." The *Daily News*'s Bob Herbert, in a wickedly funny column, disagreed. "Is it sexist?" he asked. "Oh you'd better believe it." In his article "Unsophisticated Ladies," he wrote, "The thing shows nine completely naked women with a baby grand piano and an elegantly dressed Duke Ellington standing on their heads." For good measure, Herbert added an unforgettable analogy: "This monstrosity... looks like a giant bowling trophy."[155]

Despite concerns about its appropriateness, the Duke Ellington Monument was ultimately unveiled on July 1, 1997. It was the first, and remains the only, figurative statue of a Black musician in New York City. The dedication, coming some eighteen years after Bobby Short first

Duke Ellington Memorial "caryatids." *New York Public Design Commission.*

proposed the monument, was a tribute to both his determination and the challenge of getting things done in New York City. "I hope," Short said, "my efforts will do justice to the memory of Duke Ellington." Both Short and Wynton Marsalis serenaded the crowd with Ellington music. Three New York mayors, Ed Koch, David Dinkins and Rudy Giuliani, were on hand for the proceedings at Duke Ellington Circle in the northeast corner of Central Park at 110th Street and 5th Avenue.[156] The site, previously Frawley Circle, had been renamed two years prior in preparation. The location, Short explained, served both as a gateway to Ellington's beloved Harlem and a link between "Ellington's two worlds: the sophistication of the Upper East Side and the street of Harlem."[157]

Left: Civil War Soldiers' Monument, Henry Jackson Ellicott, 1876. *David Jacobs.*

Below: Detail, Civil War Soldiers' Monument, Henry Jackson Ellicott, 1876. *David Jacobs.*

Top: Henry Ward Beecher Monument, John Quincy Adams Ward, 1891. *David Jacobs.*

Bottom: Navy Group, Soldiers' and Sailors' Memorial Arch, Frederick MacMonnies, 1892. *David Jacobs.*

Right: *Africa*, *The Four Continents*, Daniel Chester French, 1907. *David Jacobs.*

Below: Emancipation panel, Carl Schurz Memorial, Karl Bitter, 1913. *David Jacobs*.

Right: Henry Ward Beecher Memorial, Gutzon Borglum, 1914. *David Jacobs.*

Below: Marquis de Lafayette Memorial, Daniel Chester French, 1917. *David Jacobs.*

Above, left: *Woman, the Mother and Housekeeper*, Heinz Warneke, 1938. *National Archives.*

Above, right: *Man, the Provider*, Heinz Warneke, 1938. *National Archives.*

Left: *Cotton* figure in *Industries of the British Empire*, Carl Paul Jennewein, 1933. *David Jacobs.*

Exodus and Dance, Richmond Barthé, 1941. *David Jacobs.*

Top: Colonel William Hayward memorial plaque, Selma Burke, 1945. *Author photo.*

Bottom: Bust of Booker T. Washington, Richmond Barthé, 1946. *Author photo.*

Top: *Lincoln and Child*, Charles Keck, 1949. *David Jacobs.*

Bottom: Coast Guard memorial, Norman Thomas, 1955. *David Jacobs*.

Above, left: Young George Washington Carver, by Robert Amendola, 1955. *David Jacobs.*

Above, right: Dr. Martin Luther King Jr. Memorial, Stan Sawyer, 1970. *David Jacobs*.

Left: George Washington Carver, by Richmond Barthé, 1977. *David Jacobs.*

Left: Jackie Robinson Monument, Inge Hardison, 1981. *David Jacobs.*

Below: Reverend Benjamin J. Lowry Monument, Robert W. Pugh, 1982. *David Jacobs.*

Top: Dr. Ronald E. McNair Monument, Ogundipe Fayomi, 1994. *David Jacobs.*

Bottom: Duke Ellington Memorial, Robert Graham, 1997. *David Jacobs.*

Peter and Willie statue, Otto Neals, 1997. *David Jacobs.*

Top: *Soul in Flight*, Arthur Ashe memorial, Eric Fischl, 2001. *David Jacobs.*

Bottom: *Invisible Man: A Memorial to Ralph Ellison*, Elizabeth Catlett, 2003. *David Jacobs*.

Top: *Higher Ground*: The Adam Clayton Powell Jr. Memorial, Branly Cadet, 2005. *David Jacobs*.

Bottom: Jackie Robinson and Pee Wee Reese Monument, William Behrends, 2005. *David Jacobs.*

Clockwise from top left: *Swing Low*: The Harriet Tubman Memorial, Alison Saar, 2007; Frederick Douglass Memorial, Gabriel Koren and Algernon Miller, 2011; Women's Rights Pioneers Monument, Meredith Bergman, 2020; Althea Gibson Monument, Eric Goulder, 2019. *David Jacobs.*

Chapter 23

SOUL IN FLIGHT: A MEMORIAL TO ARTHUR ASHE

Soul in Flight, Arthur Ashe memorial, Eric Fischl, 2001. *David Jacobs.*

SCULPTOR: Eric Fischl (1948–)
DEDICATED: August 28, 2000
LOCATION: Billie Jean King National Tennis Center, Flushing Meadows-Corona Park, Queens
ARCHITECT: Mark Sullivan
MATERIALS: Bronze, Granite
SIZE: Figure H: 14'
DONOR: USTA

Inscription:

> *FROM WHAT WE GET, WE CAN MAKE A LIVING; WHAT WE GIVE, HOWEVER, MAKES A LIFE.*

"This is awful," cried a woman in the crowd, when *Soul in Flight*, a memorial to Arthur Ashe, was unveiled at the 2000 U.S. Open. The woman was Emily Moore, founder of the Junior Tennis Alliance in Roosevelt, Long Island, and according to *New York Newsday*, she added, "This is not what Arthur was about. Where are the books? Where are the children? Kids will see that and what will they think?"[158] Former United States Tennis Association (USTA) president Judy Levering, who spent years making the sculpture a reality, will never forget this first very public critique. To Levering's dismay, Moore and many others were upset because the memorial intended to honor tennis legend Arthur Ashe bore no resemblance to him. Not only did the fourteen-foot bronze statue of a young, muscular Black man serving a tennis ball look nothing like Ashe—he was also naked. Responding to the criticism, Levering told the *New York Times*, "The sculpture is not a depiction of Arthur; it is a representation honoring his legacy and memory."[159] Much of the public didn't seem to get it. "Whoever heard of playing tennis without any clothes?" one attendee asked the *Los Angeles Times*. Some even started a petition to have the offending sculpture removed.[160] And yet it stayed.

Soul in Flight was just one of many ways in which the USTA sought to honor the memory of tennis legend and humanitarian Arthur Ashe following his death in 1993 at age forty-nine. Ashe died of complications from AIDS, which he contracted from a blood transfusion he received during heart bypass surgery. Despite his illness, he established the Arthur Ashe Foundation for the Defeat of AIDS and spent the final year of his life raising awareness about the disease, often in vulnerable urban communities. In 1997, as part of a major renovation of the National Tennis Center in Queens, home to the U.S. Open, the USTA named what was and remains the world's largest tennis stadium after Ashe, the first and only Black man to ever win singles titles at the U.S. Open (in 1968), the Australian Open (in 1970) and Wimbledon (in 1975). Off the court, Ashe was a tireless civil rights activist known for his long battle against apartheid in South Africa. In an interview with the author, USTA president Levering recalled that the USTA Board considered naming the arena USTA Stadium or even after a corporate sponsor. But the idea of naming it for a tennis great also came up, and Levering proposed Ashe because he was, she said, "a champion in

Arthur Ashe playing in the 1975 ABN World Tennis Tournament, Rotterdam, Netherlands. *Public domain.*

tennis and more importantly a champion in life." The board, which included former Mayor David Dinkins, unanimously agreed.[161]

Levering said that when Arthur Ashe stadium opened in 1997, several people approached her and asked, "Where's the statue?" It seems tennis fans assumed at a stadium named after Ashe, there would naturally be a statue in his honor. Responding to public demand, Levering formed a memorial committee cochaired by former Sotheby's CEO Michael Ainslie and Ashe's widow, Jeanne Moutoussammy-Ashe. In an interview with the author, Ainslie recalled asking fans and friends of Ashe to each donate $25,000. He later proudly recalled hitting their target, $1 million, within a month.[162] The donors' names are engraved on a plaque affixed to the retaining wall of the commemorative garden. Inscribed in the wall is a quote from Ashe: "From what we get, we make a living; what we give, however, makes a life."

The sculpture at the center of all the fuss was the work of renowned artist Eric Fischl. Fischl, whom the *Times* described as "an agreeably rumpled fellow," explained to the press and repeated later in his memoir, *Bad Boy*, that he wanted to represent the spirit and energy of Ashe without doing a "Disney-like…portrait" of him, like a statue that had been done in Ashe's hometown, Richmond.[163] Also aiming for a piece that wouldn't be dated by fashion, Fischl made the piece nude in the classical tradition. He chose a serving pose because, as he wrote, "It seemed to work as wordplay—to *serve* the greater community. But, I also think it's the game's most beautiful stroke." Ashe's widow, who, as a memorial committee member, approved Fischl's concept, released a statement through the USTA responding to the public uproar: "I believe he [Ashe] would approve of this commemorative statue." Aware of the significance of a rare public statue of a Black man in New York, she added, "I am also pleased that the figure celebrates the life of an African-American man in a park that serves an incredible mosaic of ethnic groups in this great city."[164]

This was not the first time that a memorial to Arthur Ashe was the center of controversy. In 1996, protestors waving Confederate flags picketed the groundbreaking of a statue to him on Monument Avenue in Richmond, Virginia. Richmond was where Ashe first learned to play tennis as a child, on segregated courts in a park where his father was the caretaker. The protesters objected, it seems, to the tennis pioneer and civil rights activist joining Lost Cause heroes like Jefferson Davis, Stonewall Jackson and Robert E. Lee. Others felt it was wrong to include Ashe in Confederate company, including Moutoussammy-Ashe, who, in an editorial in the *Richmond Times-Dispatch*, suggested the Richmond Sports Hall of Fame as an alternate location.[165] Nonetheless, a twelve-foot bronze by Paul DiPasquale of Ashe in a sweatsuit, somewhat awkwardly holding a tennis racket in one hand and three books in the other, broke the color barrier on Monument Avenue on July 10, 1996, what would have been Ashe's fifty-third birthday.

Following the murder of George Floyd in 2020, the Black mayor of Richmond, Levar Stoney, ordered the monuments to Davis, Jackson, Lee and other Confederates on city property removed: the monument to Ashe remains.[166] And despite early resistance, so does *Soul in Flight*, which fans eventually warmed to. Now, during the U.S. Open tournament, families line up to have their picture taken in front of the sculpture—even with their children.

Chapter 24

INVISIBLE MAN: A MEMORIAL TO RALPH ELLISON

Invisible Man: A Memorial to Ralph Ellison, Elizabeth Catlett, 2003. *David Jacobs.*

SCULPTOR: Elizabeth Catlett (1915–2012)
DEDICATED: May 1, 2003
LOCATION: 150th Street and Riverside Drive
ARCHITECT: Ken Smith, landscape architect
MATERIALS: Bronze and Deer Isle granite
SIZE: H × W × D: 15' × 7'6" × 6"
Weight: 5,000 pounds
DONOR: Riverside Park Fund and Ralph Ellison Memorial Committee

Inscription 1:

> *Ralph Ellison, 1914–1994, American writer. Longtime resident of 730 Riverside Drive. His pioneering novel Invisible Man (1952) details the struggles of a young African-American man in a hostile society.*

Inscription 2:

> *"I am an invisible man….I am invisible, understand, simply because people refuse to see me."—Ralph Ellison, 1952*
> *Invisible Man, Elizabeth Catlett, Sculptor, May 2003*

Inscription 3:

> *"The very idea of being in New York was dreamlike, for like many young negroes of the time, I thought of it as the freest of American cities, and considered Harlem as the site and symbol of Afro-American progress and hope. Indeed, I was both young and bookish enough to think of Manhattan as my substitute for Paris, and of Harlem as a place of Left Bank excitement. So now that I was there in its glamorous scene, I meant to make the most of its opportunities."—Ralph Ellison, "An Extravagance of Laughter," 1986*

From May through September, one can enjoy Jazz in the Park in Harlem's Ralph Ellison Plaza and also take in Invisible Man: A Memorial to Ralph Ellison. These delightful concerts are something Ralph Ellison himself would undoubtedly have enjoyed, because he loved the park and he loved jazz. In fact, he studied trumpet at the Tuskegee Institute until he moved to New York in 1936 to try his hand at sculpting and earn some money for school. Ellison soon fell in love with what he later described as the "freest of American cities," and his experiences there, removed from the segregated South, sharpened his views on the United States' color line.

A chance meeting with Langston Hughes at the Harlem YMCA opened up a world of Black literary figures to Ellison. In 1938, he met Richard Wright, who encouraged him to write and helped him get a job at the New Deal New York Writers' Project, interviewing for and writing its study *The Negro in New York.*[167] During World War II, he was a cook in the U.S. Merchant Marine, and he returned home eager to continue writing. His first novel, *Invisible Man*, was published in 1952 to great acclaim. The

A lovely June day in Ralph Ellison Plaza. *David Jacobs.*

groundbreaking work of fiction and winner of the National Book Award chronicles the peculiar, at times hilarious, at times horrifying experience of a young Black man trying to find his identity in New York during the Depression. Ellison's subsequent work never equaled the popular success of his first book, but he continued to write and publish. He also taught Russian and American literature at Bard College and creative writing at Rutgers University, and from 1970 to 1980, he was the Albert Schweitzer Professor of Humanities at New York University.[168] For over forty years, he lived with his wife, Fanny, in the Beaumont Apartments at 370 Riverside Drive, also home to the singer Marian Anderson. Ellison's neighbors remembered him as a friendly gentleman who gave away signed copies of his work and liked to stop and chat.[169]

In 1998, a few years after Ellison died of pancreatic cancer at age eighty, one of his Beaumont neighbors, Anne Dobson, launched a campaign to honor him with a statue in the traffic island across the street from the building, a place where the author would often sit and enjoy the view of the Hudson. Dobson formed a memorial committee chaired by architect and Harlem historian John Reddick, and they partnered with the Riverside Park

Left: Ralph Ellison, undated photo. *Wikimedia Commons.*

Right: Elizabeth Catlett (*center*) in Mexico in the 1940s with her mother (*left*) and her husband, Francisco Mora (*right*). *New York Public Library.*

Conservancy to raise money and support for the project. With the approval of the Department of Parks and Recreation and Councilman Stanley Michaels as a champion, the project moved forward. In a conversation with the author, Reddick explained that, when it came to the memorial concept, the committee, which included Ellison's widow, Fanny, chose to avoid a literal representation. A design competition for the project followed, and the unanimous choice of the conservancy and the committee was the renowned African American printmaker and sculptor Elizabeth Catlett.[170]

"A big black rectangle with a hole in it" is how Elizabeth Catlett described her *Invisible Man* memorial in an interview with *Ebony Magazine*. But it's so much more. A literal reference to the book, the fifteen-foot-tall, five-thousand-pound bronze monolith features the silhouette of a striding Black man. Catlett's design responds to a famous quote from the book's epilogue, which is inscribed on one of the granite panels by the statue, "I am an invisible man…I am invisible, understand, simply because people refuse to see me." Catlett's elegant answer to Ellison's statement is to make the man people refuse to see visible. This sculpture, Catlett's only public work in the city, was a natural addition to her remarkable career spent bringing to light the lives of primarily Black and Mexican women. Like Ellison, Catlett was devoted to making the invisible visible.

The child of teachers, Catlett grew up in Washington, D.C., during the Depression and was attuned to the cruelties of both class and racism. An artist from an early age, she was accepted at Carnegie Mellon University on the strength of her portfolio, only to be rejected when the school discovered

Elizabeth Catlett at *Invisible Man* dedication, next to John Reddick (*on her left*). *Spencer T. Tucker Photo. NYC Parks/Art and Antiquities.*

she was Black. Instead, she studied art at Howard University, where she was influenced by the teaching of Alain Locke, a great champion of Black art. In 1940, Catlett became the first African American to earn an MFA in sculpture from the University of Iowa. After teaching for a time in Harlem at the Carver School for adult education, where she met Ralph Ellison, she traveled to Mexico in 1946 on a Rosenwald Grant, where she was inspired by artists like Diego Rivera who were doing "murals, and prints, public art… for the people of Mexico." Catlett settled in Mexico, got married, raised a family and became a Mexican citizen. Still, she never lost sight of the United States and the injustices there.[171] Catlett was a feminist and a civil rights activist, and her work reflected her personal sense of responsibility to Black people. "I have always wanted my art to service black people," she told art historian Samella Lewis, "to reflect us, to relate to us, to stimulate us, to make us aware of our potential."[172]

When Ellison's memorial was unveiled on May 1, 2003, eighty-eight-year-old Catlett was there, sitting on a bench dedicated to her late husband, Mexican painter Francisco Mora. Ellison's widow, Fanny, was there too. Overcome with emotion, she wept during the ceremony. There were readings from Ellison's work, punctuated by music, including the "Negro National Anthem." Also present were singer and civil rights icon Odetta and actress Ruby Dee. "I love it," Dee told *Jet Magazine*. "It's an Invisible Man you can't help but recognize."[173]

"Art in public spaces," Catlett once wrote, "is only valid when it has some relationship to the community. It is not good enough to be merely functional or even beautiful. We must also meet the psychological and social needs of our people."[174] Today, the small plaza outside 370 Riverside Drive is a living memorial to a cherished neighbor, a hub where friends gather, musicians play and volunteers tend to the garden. Looking through the *Invisible Man* silhouette, one sees the Harlem neighborhood Ellison knew and the people he loved. One imagines he would approve.

Chapter 25

HIGHER GROUND: THE ADAM CLAYTON POWELL JR. MEMORIAL

Higher Ground: The Adam Clayton Powell Jr. Memorial, 2005. *David Jacobs.*

SCULPTOR: Branly Cadet (1966–)
DEDICATED: February 17, 2005
LOCATION: Adam Clayton Powell Jr. Boulevard and 125th Street
MEDIUM: Sculpture: Bronze
Base: Stainless steel and black granite
SIZE: H: 11'
DONOR: Multiple private individuals and businesses

Inscription:

South side:

Press forward at all times climbing toward that higher ground of the harmonious society that shapes the laws of man to the laws of God.

North side:

Keep the Faith

Contrary to popular belief, the battles of the Civil Rights Movement weren't fought only in the South. They were also fought in the North, in the 1930s, when Harlem was the cultural capital of Black America and Black Harlemites faced discrimination in their own neighborhood. On the main thoroughfare of 125th Street, Black people shopped in white-owned stores like Woolworths where they weren't allowed to work and rode on city buses that only white men were hired to drive. To Adam Clayton Powell Jr., the young pastor of Abyssinian Baptist Church, this was intolerable.

Powell was a once-in-a-generation leader who confronted racism head-on, a larger-than-life character with a flair for the dramatic. His *New York Times* obituary described him as a "political demagogue…a wheelerdealer, a rabble-rouser, a grandstander, a fugitive" and "a playboy." Late in Powell's life, when he was in exile in the Bahamas, a *Times* reporter asked him if he had any advice for his supporters. Powell, holding a glass of Cutty Sark with milk and puffing on his signature cigar, replied in his raspy preacher voice, "Tell them I said, 'Keep the faith, baby; spread it gently and walk together, children.'"[175]

Born in 1908 into a family of Black elites, Powell had hazel eyes, fair skin and straight hair. He often passed as white, including during his first year in college at Colgate, but ultimately chose to identify as Black. In 1937, after succeeding his father in the pulpit, Powell, a charismatic and electrifying speaker, mobilized his congregation of over ten thousand, one of the largest Black churches in the United States, to fight discrimination. Deploying tactics that Martin Luther King Jr. would later use in Montgomery, Alabama, Powell led a nonviolent "Don't Buy Where You Can't Work" campaign, boycotting stores and buses and pressuring utilities and hospitals until thousands of Black people were given jobs.[176] According to his eldest son, Adam Clayton Powell III, Powell boasted he had Black people working in all the stores on 125th Street except one restaurant, Franks, because, as he joked, "There should be one place in Harlem where Black people could go to eat, and be waited on by whites."[177]

Despite his contributions to the Civil Rights Movement both from the pulpit and in Congress, the thrice married Powell developed a reputation for womanizing and corruption. He eventually ran into legal trouble and was accused of tax evasion and misappropriating public funds. Following a House investigation into his conduct in 1967, he was temporarily excluded from his seat, and to pay for his mounting legal bills, he released both a book and a captivating live album of his fiery sermons titled *Keep the Faith, Baby!* During this time, he spent much of his time on the island of Bimini in the Bahamas with a woman (not his wife), Corinne Huff, a former Miss Ohio.[178] In 1970, he lost the House seat he'd held for eleven consecutive terms to Charles Rangel. In 1972, he died in Miami of cancer at age sixty-three. In Harlem, thousands lined up to pay their final respects to Powell at Abyssinian Baptist Church.[179]

Not long after Powell's death, in 1974, Harlem City Councilman Fred Samuel pushed through a local law that renamed 7th Avenue between Central Park North and 155th Street Adam Clayton Powell Jr. Boulevard. This began a trend in Harlem that would inspire the renaming of three boulevards after Frederick Douglass, Martin Luther King Jr. and Malcolm X.[180] In 1983, the State Office Building at 125th and Adam Clayton Powell Jr. Boulevard was renamed in Powell's honor after the passage of a bill introduced by Harlem Assemblywoman Geraldine Daniels. "I don't care what happened in the later stages of his life," said Daniels. "He was monumental in what happened right here on 125th Street."[181]

In 1996, Dr. Will Brown Jr., an African American real estate broker with a doctorate in management philosophy, was appointed by Republican Governor George Pataki to manage the Powell Building. In an interview with the author, Brown recalled, his first day on the job, being struck by the empty plaza in front of the building that, he thought, was crying out for a memorial of some kind. Brown formed a memorial committee that, under his guidance, quickly decided it should be a memorial to Adam Clayton Powell Jr. Brown, a great admirer of Powell and his message that the power to change things and make things better was "in your hands," led a campaign that raised over $300,000 from private donors and businesses to pay for the memorial. It was a bipartisan effort, with Democrats Charles Rangel and David Patterson helping to solicit donations and the support of the Harlem community, while Republican Governor Pataki chipped in

$2 million from the state to cover construction costs. Brown formed an artist selection committee to find artists from the community, and Branly Cadet was chosen.

Born and raised in New York, of Haitian descent, Cadet studied sculpting at Cornell and the New York Academy of Art and apprenticed with the sculptor Martine Vaugel in France. His only known work at the time was a bronze medallion of William Shakespeare on a residential building at Twenty-Third Street and Sixth Avenue marking the spot where Booth's theater, built by noted Shakespearian actor Edwin Booth, once stood. Cadet was chosen on the strength of his proposal and his heritage. In a conversation with the author, Cadet recalled being thrilled with the opportunity to sculpt Powell, because Cadet felt like he was a direct beneficiary of Powell's work. As he said, "I wanted to honor the legacy of important American figures who were African American."[182] Since his work on the Powell memorial, Cadet has created a number of other remarkable public works depicting African Americans, including a sculpture of the nineteenth-century civil rights activist Octavius Cato in front of Philadelphia's City Hall and Jackie Robinson sliding into home outside Dodger Stadium in Los Angeles.

In the *Higher Ground* memorial, Cadet portrays Powell as an eleven-foot bronze giant, earnestly striding uphill, his coattails billowing in the headwind, reminiscent of a certain Caped Crusader from Gotham. Cadet's work at once conveys the Sisyphean challenge of fighting for civil rights and Powell's determination to win. It embodies the quote from one of Powell's sermons etched on the south side of the stainless steel base, "Press forward at all times climbing toward that higher ground of the harmonious society that shapes the laws of man to the laws of God."

In Powell's right hand, he grips a congressional record, a symbol of his long, remarkable career as a politician. He became the first Black man elected to the New York City Council in 1941 and, soon after, the first Black man to represent New York City in Congress, which he did from 1944 to 1970. Engraved on the base of the memorial is a list of Powell's efforts to end discrimination, starting with the institution of Congress itself, where he brazenly used "whites only" facilities like the House restaurant, the House gym and the Congressional barbershop. When Powell learned that John Rankin, a segregationist representative from Mississippi, didn't want to sit near Black House members, Powell went out of his way to sit next to him, once following him from seat to seat five times. "The only people with whom [Rankin] is qualified to sit," Powell said, "are Hitler and Mussolini."[183] Relentless in his assault on racism, Powell held accommodationist Black leaders in contempt, saying, "During past years, like frightened children, we were afraid to eat the strong meat of human rights and instead sucked the milk of civil rights from the breasts of white liberals, black Uncle Toms and Aunt Jemimas."[184]

Inscribed on the north side of the base is Powell's catchphrase, "Keep the faith" (minus the *baby* for artistic reasons, three words being more symmetrical and easier to engrave than four), superimposed on top of a list of all the bills he proposed and all the causes he fought for while in Congress, including equal pay for women, expanding the minimum wage and ending school segregation.[185] Among his greatest achievements in office was drafting what became known as the Powell Amendment, which proposed to block federal funding for any institution that practiced racial discrimination. This, as well as legislation proposed by Powell to make lynching a federal crime and to ban the southern poll tax on Black voters, became part of the landmark 1964 Civil Rights Act.

The memorial unveiling took place on a cold February day in 2005. Mayor Bloomberg, Governor Pataki and Charles Rangel attended. Powell's family was represented by his two sons from his second and third marriages, Adam Clayton Powell III, a television producer, and Adam Clayton Powell IV, a state assemblyman from Harlem. Speaking to the crowd, Powell IV said, "This is a great day long overdue.…Too many of our young people do not know about Adam Clayton Powell."[186] Will Brown Jr., who had spent over seven years shepherding the memorial to completion, recalled the most rewarding part of the project coming at one in the morning after the dedication when he received a call from Powell IV, "Guess where I am?" he asked, "I'm standing here in front of the statue, and I'm standing here with tears in my eyes."[187]

Chapter 26

JACKIE ROBINSON AND PEE WEE REESE MONUMENT

Jackie Robinson and Pee Wee Reese Monument, William Behrends, 2005. *David Jacobs.*

SCULPTOR: William Behrends (1946–)
DEDICATED: November 1, 2005
LOCATION: In front of Maimonides Park, Brooklyn Cyclones Stadium, Coney Island
ARCHITECT: Ken Smith Landscape Architects
MEDIUM: Bronze, granite
DONOR: Multiple donors

Inscription:

> *IN MAY 1947, ON CINCINNATI'S CROSLEY FIELD, ROBINSON ENDURED RACIST TAUNTS, JEERS, AND DEATH THREATS THAT WOULD HAVE BROKEN THE SPIRIT OF A LESSER MAN.*
>
> *REESE, CAPTAIN OF THE BROOKLYN DODGERS, WALKED OVER TO HIS TEAMMATE ROBINSON AND STOOD BY HIS SIDE, SILENCING THE TAUNTS OF THE CROWD.*
>
> *THIS SIMPLE GESTURE CHALLENGED PREJUDICE AND CREATED A POWERFUL AND ENDURING FRIENDSHIP.*
>
> *BORN 1919, CAIRO, GEORGIA, DIED 1972, STAMFORD, CONNECTICUT, JACK ROOSEVELT ROBINSON, 42. ON APRIL 15, 1947, ROBINSON FIRST TOOK THE FIELD FOR THE BROOKLYN DODGERS, BREAKING THE COLOR BARRIER IN MAJOR LEAGUE BASEBALL. IN THE FACE OF HOSTILITY, HE REMAINED STEADFAST, WINNING HIS WAY INTO THE HALL OF FAME AND THE HEARTS OF BASEBALL FANS. ROBINSON WAS A CHAMPION OF THE GAME OF BASEBALL, OF JUSTICE, AND OF CIVIL RIGHTS.*
>
> *CITY OF NEW YORK, PARKS & RECREATION. MICHAEL R. BLOOMBERG, MAYOR. ADRIAN BENEPE, COMMISSIONER. THE MAYOR'S FUND TO ADVANCE NEW YORK CITY. WILLIAM BEHRENDS, SCULPTOR, 2005.*
>
> *BORN 1918, EKRON, KENTUCKY, DIED 1999, LOUISVILLE, KENTUCKY, HAROLD HENRY REESE, 1. KNOWN AS PEE WEE, REESE WAS CAPTAIN OF THE BROOKLYN DODGERS DURING THE LATE 1940s AND THE EARLY 1950s. HE RISKED HIS CAREER WHEN HE STOOD BY JACKIE ROBINSON AGAINST PREJUDICED FANS AND FELLOW PLAYERS. WITH THIS ACT OF DEFIANCE, THE HALL OF FAME SHORTSTOP BECAME A POWERFUL AND INFLUENTIAL MODEL OF TRUE HUMANITY.*

> *I hope you bust the league wide open with base hits this year. Good luck. You're a credit to all races: or better, to the human race.*
>
> *Signed, Gordon Brooks*
>
> *P.S. A "Bum" fan, and a white man*[188]

This is one of many letters of support that Jackie Robinson received after he broke major league baseball's color barrier on April 15, 1947. Many fans, Black and white, wanted him to succeed. But many, in the segregated nation, weren't ready for a Black man in the national pastime. In his rookie year, Robinson received death threats, and threatening letters telling him to "get out of baseball."[189] His Dodger teammate Dixie Walker circulated a player petition against him joining the team and, when that failed, requested a trade. Members of the St. Louis Cardinals threatened to strike rather than share the field with a Black player.[190] On the road, Robinson was subjected to taunts from both players and fans. His treatment was especially bad at Cincinnati's Crosley Field, one of the southernmost ballparks in the league, just across the border from Kentucky.

During the first game of a road series against the Reds, an incident occurred that would go down in baseball lore. While there is no footage of the game, and neither the Black nor the white press recorded anything unusual, some players later recalled that when the Dodgers took the field in the first inning, fans unleashed a torrent of abuse at Robinson, who was playing first base. Pee Wee Reese, the Dodger captain and shortstop, came over to Robinson, put his arm around his shoulders and silenced the crowd. The fact that Reese was from Kentucky may have helped. This simple act of empathy is what the sculptor William Behrends attempted to realistically capture in his Jackie Robinson and Pee Wee Reese Monument outside Maimonides Park, home of the Coney Island Cyclones.

Shortly after Pee Wee Reese's death at age eighty-one, the idea to make his legendary gesture a monument emerged from a memorial service at Saint Patrick's Church in Bay Ridge. The source was Stan Isaacs, a retired white sports writer from *Newsday* who had covered the Dodgers. Isaacs grew up in Brooklyn a Giant fan, but switched to the Dodgers because, as he later told the *Daily News*, "I couldn't root against the Dodgers after Jackie got there because every bigot in the country was rooting against him."[191] Before a church full of hundreds of old Dodger fans, Isaacs considered how to properly honor Brooklyn's beloved captain and Hall of Famer: "I would be hesitant to name a highway after him. It's no great thrill to hear the radio reports of a backup on the Jackie Robinson Parkway."[192] Instead, Isaacs suggested memorializing the moment when Reese stood up for Robinson in the face of racism.

The *New York Post*'s Jack Newfield, a white reporter, wrote about Isaacs' idea in his column, which caught the attention of another Brooklyn native, New York City Mayor Rudolph Giuliani. By December 1999, the baseball-loving Giuliani had announced the formation of a special committee to raise private funds, choose the sculptor and find a location for the Robinson and Reese monument. The cost of the statue was estimated at $1 million. Private equity pioneer and lifelong Dodger fan Ted Forstmann quickly launched the fundraising drive with $100,000; the Mets, the Yankees and Major League Baseball soon pledged the same amount.[193] The remainder of the funds came from individuals and businesses, whose names are engraved on a stone tablet adjacent to the monument.

On the morning of September 11, 2001, the statue selection committee was at New York City Hall about to hear monument proposals, in a meeting that the mayor was scheduled to attend, when the planes hit the World Trade Center. According to Suzanne Randolph, the creative consultant who guided the selection process, the debris from the collapse of the towers kept the committee, which included Robinson's widow, Rachel, and Reese's widow, Dottie, trapped for much of the day in a safe area in city hall.[194] The terrorist attack and the change of administration delayed the project for two years, and it wasn't until the winter of 2003 that Mayor Michael R. Bloomberg, also a baseball fan, revived it. From a field of eight sculptors, two of whom were African American, the committee chose a white sculptor, William Behrends, known then for his statue of Willie Mays outside San Francisco's Oracle Park and, more recently, for his statue of Tom Seaver at the main entrance of Citi Field.[195] The committee also decided to locate the memorial at KeySpan Park (now Maimonides Park), where, in 2001, for the first time since the Dodgers left in 1957, the Cyclones brought professional baseball back to Brooklyn.

On November 1, 2005, just over fifty years after the 1955 Dodgers won Brooklyn's only World Series, the Jackie Robinson and Pee Wee Reese Monument was unveiled with their widows in attendance, along with hundreds of fans. Many speakers portrayed Reese in heroic terms, but Dottie Reese saw it differently: "For him, it was a simple gesture of friendship. He had no idea that it would become so significant." As for her husband's reaction, Rachel Robinson remembered, "It came as such a relief to him that a teammate and the captain of the team would go out of his way in such a public fashion to express friendship."[196]

Since the dedication of the monument, many sports writers and historians have raised questions about the moment it supposedly represents and when and where it took place. Some point to the fact that because Robinson was a first baseman in 1947, it would have been a longer and more awkward walk for the shortstop Reese than when Robinson moved to second base in

Jackie Robinson and Pee Wee Reese Monument in Coney Island. *David Jacobs.*

1948. Some argue it's more likely that the event took place that year because Robinson and Reese didn't truly become firm friends until they were double-play partners.[197] Perhaps most importantly, Robinson himself remembered in his autobiography that the incident occurred in Boston in 1948 when the Dodgers were playing against the Braves, not in Cincinnati.[198] His teammate Duke Snider had a similar recollection.[199]

Regardless of the details of the moment, the monument appears to show a greater truth: that Pee Wee Reese stood up for his friend, Jackie Robinson. It is, in fact, the only portrait statue in New York City that honors a personal friendship between a Black man and a white man. Reese appears on the same level as Robinson—a friend and an ally to the hero who broke the color line. As Robinson later recalled, "He didn't say a word, but he looked over at the chaps who were yelling at me and just stared. He was standing by me, I could tell you that."[200]

Chapter 27

SWING LOW: THE HARRIET TUBMAN MEMORIAL

Swing Low: The Harriet Tubman Memorial, Alison Saar, 2007. *David Jacobs.*

SCULPTOR: Alison Saar (1956–)
DEDICATED: November 13, 2008
LOCATION: West 122nd Street, Saint Nicholas Avenue and Frederick Douglass Boulevard
ARCHITECT: Quennell Rothschild Partners (landscape design)
MEDIUM: Bronze, Chinese granite
DIMENSIONS: Approx. H × L: 13' × 14'
DONOR: Percent for Art, New York City Department of Cultural Affairs

Inscription:

HARRIET TUBMAN MEMORIAL
ALISON SAAR
SWING LOW, 2007
PLAZA DESIGN IN COLLABORATION WITH
QUENNELL ROTHSCHILD & PARTNERS LLP
COMMISSIONED BY THE CITY OF NEW YORK
MANHATTAN BOROUGH PRESIDENT'S OFFICE
DEPARTMENT OF CULTURAL AFFAIRS PERCENT FOR ART PROGRAM
DEPARTMENT OF PARKS & RECREATION
DEPARTMENT OF TRANSPORTATION
DEPARTMENT OF DESIGN AND CONSTRUCTION

The first public statue in New York City honoring a Black woman can be found on a small traffic triangle in Harlem at the intersection of 122nd Street, Saint Nicholas Avenue and Frederick Douglass Boulevard. Here, across the street from the New York Police Department's Twenty-Eighth Precinct, the drama of Harriet Tubman's legendary life unfolds on a thirteen-foot bronze sculpture by the Black artist Alison Saar. Tubman was born into slavery on Maryland's Eastern Shore around 1822. When she was thirteen, a slave owner, trying to stop an enslaved boy from escaping, accidently hit her in the head with a two-pound weight. It took Tubman months to recover from the blow, and she suffered from headaches and seizures for the rest of her life. During these spells, she had visions that deepened her faith in God and her determination to be free.[201]

When she was twenty-seven, Tubman, who had no children, made a bold decision to leave her family and her husband, John Tubman, a free Black man, behind and escape to Philadelphia. "When I found I had crossed that line," Tubman later recalled, "I looked at my hands to see if I was the same person. There was such a glory over everything; the sun came like gold through the trees, and over the fields, and I felt like I was in Heaven."[202] Both the accident and the escape, as well as other key episodes in her life, like her marriage and her death, are shown on bronze tiles ringing the granite base of the memorial. Interspersed among these scenes are tiles with traditional quilt panel patterns.

After her escape, instead of remaining safely in the North, Tubman became a conductor on the Underground Railroad, returning to Maryland roughly thirteen times over the next ten years to lead nearly seventeen family members

Left: Harriet Tubman between 1871 and 1876. *Library of Congress.*

Below: *Swing Low*: The Harriet Tubman Memorial, Alison Saar, 2007. *David Jacobs.*

and friends to freedom.[203] On one of these trips, Tubman came looking to bring her husband north with her, only to find that he had married another woman and did not want to go. Undaunted, Tubman found other enslaved people who wanted to escape and led them to freedom. Saar's sculpture shows the determined woman who came to be known as Black Moses on the move: looking, leaning and striding forward. Saar, who was inspired to become a sculptor by her mother and Elizabeth Catlett (see *Invisible Man* on page 133) said she wanted to show Tubman "not as the conductor of the Underground Railroad but as the train itself, an unstoppable locomotive."[204] To make this point, the artist included a train's cowcatcher below the hem of Tubman's green skirt.

In that same skirt float faces representing the people Tubman rescued from slavery and the things they brought on their escape north: keys, bottles, shackles and worn-out shoes. Trailing in Tubman's wake are a tangle of roots representing how slaves uprooted their lives to flee the South, as well as Tubman's part in uprooting slavery. Tubman continued the fight against slavery during the Civil War, serving in the Union army as a spy, a scout and a nurse in the South Carolina Sea Islands Campaign.[205] After the war, in 1868, Tubman received the ultimate tribute for her work in a personal letter from Frederick Douglass, in which he wrote, "I know of no one who has willingly encountered more perils and hardships to serve our enslaved people than you have."[206]

So how did a memorial to Harriet Tubman end up on a traffic island in Harlem? Like all New York stories, this is a real estate story. In 1999, when much of New York, including parts of Harlem, was experiencing a real estate boom, Frederick Douglass Boulevard was in decay, vacant and overlooked. Seeing an opportunity, Manhattan borough president Virginia C. Fields, an African American woman, commissioned a planning and development study for the street from 110th to 135th and gave $5 million in seed money toward improvements. The plan imagined, in addition to commercial and residential development, three statues that would serve as gateways to a rejuvenated Harlem: one of Tubman, in what would become Harriet Tubman Plaza; one of Frederick Douglass, at 110th and Central Park North; and another of Malcolm X and his wife, Dr. Betty Shabazz, at 110th and 5th Avenue.[207] In the end, Tubman and Douglass got public statues, while the building that once housed the Audubon Ballroom at Broadway and 165th Street, where Malcolm X was assassinated, became the Malcolm X and Dr. Betty Shabazz Memorial and Education Center. The lobby of the center does boast a life-size statue of the slain civil rights leader by the artist Gabriel Koren, known for her statue of Frederick Douglass.

Funding for the $2.8 million Tubman memorial project came from the Percent for Art program, which chose artist Alison Saar to sculpt the piece and landscape designers Quennell Rothschild and Partners to renovate the formerly barren triangle. The firm chose roughhewn granite along with trees and grass from both New York and Tubman's native Maryland to represent the natural landscape braved by Tubman and her passengers. The memorial and the plaza redesign won a Public Design Commission Award for Excellence in Design in 2004.[208]

And yet not everyone was pleased with the sculpture, in particular with the direction it was facing: south. Many wondered: How could the city possibly point Tubman, a woman renowned for leading people to freedom in the North, the wrong way? Before the memorial dedication on November 13, 2008, Jacob Morris, director of the Harlem Historical Society, told the *New York Times* that there was a petition with more than one thousand signatures from people in the neighborhood calling for an about-face. "We are serious, " Morris said. "We hate what they did. It is just an outrage." In response to the criticism, Saar said, "She's best known for sojourns north, but what is most impressive to me are her trips south, where she risked her own freedom."[209] It's also worth noting that, in the northern hemisphere, a south-facing statue gets better light on its face throughout the day than a north-facing one. Despite the fracas, Tubman remained southbound.

Perhaps those upset by the way the statue was facing should have also been concerned with some of the myths about Tubman and the Underground Railroad that made it into the memorial. Saar chose the title, *Swing Low*, from the African American spiritual "Swing Low, Sweet Chariot," which promises a better life in heaven, because it was believed by some to be among Tubman's favorite songs and to contain coded messages used by the Underground Railroad. However, this song wasn't written until after the Civil War, so it could not have been sung by Tubman at that time.[210] Likewise, Saar made some of the bronze tiles ringing the base reminiscent of quilt panels to represent so-called freedom quilts—quilts that some have argued contained coded messages that guided fugitive slaves to freedom. And yet there appears to be no historical evidence in support of this claim.[211] As it happens, the original plan for the Frederick Douglass monument was based on the idea of "freedom quilts" until a protest from scholars forced a change (for more on the Douglass monument, see page 155). Protests from historians aside, *Swing Low* is a work of art and not an argumentative essay.

Perhaps it's unreasonable to expect complete fidelity to facts in a public memorial, a bit like expecting historical accuracy in a Hollywood film? Why let the facts get in the way of a good story?

And that story continues. Since 2003, March 10, the anniversary of Tubman's death in 1913, has officially been Harriet Tubman Day in the state of New York. A measure of the memorial's success in honoring her is that every year at this time, the Black Women's Leadership Caucus, a group dedicated to preserving Tubman's legacy and mentoring young women, gathers around the sculpture for a wreath-laying ceremony.[212] Likewise, every year, New York City schoolchildren visit the memorial to learn her story.

Chapter 28

FREDERICK DOUGLASS MEMORIAL

Frederick Douglass Monument, Gabriel Koren and Algernon Miller, 2011. *David Jacobs.*

SCULPTOR: Gabriel Koren (figure) and Algernon Miller (1945–, site and fountain designer)
DEDICATED: September 20, 2011
LOCATION: Central Park North and Frederick Douglass Boulevard
ARCHITECT: Quennell Rothschild and Partners
MEDIUM: Bronze and granite
DONOR: Percent for Art, New York City Department of Cultural Affairs

Inscription:

Granite block 1:

BORN FREDERICK AUGUSTUS BAILEY, 1818, TALBOT COUNTY, MARYLAND.

Granite block 2:

MARRIED ANNA MURRAY IN 1838, WHO DIED IN 1882.

Granite block 3:

MARRIED HELEN PITTS IN 1884.

Granite block 4:

"WHATEVER MAY BE SAID AS TO A DIVISION OF DUTIES AND AVOCATIONS, THE RIGHTS OF MAN AND THE RIGHTS OF WOMAN ARE ONE AND INSEPARABLE, AND STAND UPON THE SAME INDESTRUCTABLE BASIS." 1851.

Granite block 5:

"THE FLIGHT WAS A BOLD AND PERILOUS ONE; BUT HERE I AM, IN THE GREAT CITY OF NEW YORK, SAFE AND SOUND, WITHOUT THE LOSS OF BLOOD OR BONE." 1855

Granite block 6:

"SUCH IS MY DETESTATION OF SLAVERY, THAT I WOULD KEEP THE MERCILESS SLAVEHOLDER PROFOUNDLY IGNORANT OF THE MEANS OF FLIGHT ADOPTED BY THE SLAVE. HE SHOULD BE LEFT TO IMAGINE HIMSELF SURROUNDED BY MYRIADS OF INVISIBLE TORMENTORS." 1855

Granite block 7:

OF MY FATHER I KNOW NOTHING. SLAVERY HAD NO RECOGNITION OF FATHERS, AS NONE OF FAMILIES." 1845

Granite block 8:

> *"IF THERE IS NO STRUGGLE THERE IS NO PROGRESS. THOSE WHO PROFESS TO FAVOR FREEDOM AND YET DEPRECATE AGITATION... WANT CROPS WITHOUT PLOWING UP THE GROUND...THEY WANT THE OCEAN WITHOUT THE AWEFUL ROAR OF ITS MANY WATERS... POWER CONCEDES NOTHING WITHOUT A DEMAND." 1857*

Pavement:

> *"RIGHT IS OF NO SEX, TRUTH IS OF NO COLOR, GOD IS THE FATHER OF US ALL, AND WE ARE ALL BRETHREN," —MASTHEAD OF THE NORTH STAR.*

Fountain, north side:

> *FREDERICK DOUGLASS, 1818–1895, BORN INTO SLAVERY IN MARYLAND, FREDERICK BAILEY FOUND THE WAY TO FREEDOM ALONG THE UNDERGROUND RAILROAD IN 1838. DISGUISED AS A SAILOR, HE TRAVELED TO MANHATTAN BY SHIP, AND FOUND SHELTER AT THE HOUSE OF ABOLITIONIST DAVID RUGGLES ON LISPENARD STREET. THERE, HE AWAITED THE ARRIVAL OF HIS FIANCEE, ANNA MURRAY, A FREE BLACK WOMAN FROM MARYLAND. THEY MARRIED, AND TOGETHER CONTINUED BAILEY'S FREEDOM JOURNEY TO MASSACHUSETTS, WHERE HE CHANGED HIS NAME TO DOUGLASS. LAUDED FOR HIS ORATION, HE BECAME A PROMINENT ABOLITIONIST AND PURCHASED HIS LEGAL FREEDOM FROM SLAVERY. PUBLISHER OF THE ABOLITIONIST JOURNAL THE NORTH STAR, HE CHAMPIONED FREEDOM FOR ALL AMERICANS AND ENDORSED WOMEN'S SUFFRAGE. DOUGLASS LATER HELD POSTS AS ASSISTANT SECRETARY OF THE SANTO DOMINGO COMMISSION (1871), MARSHALL OF THE DISTRICT OF COLUMBIA (1877–1881) AND U.S. MINISTER TO HAITI (1889–1891). FOLLOWING THE DEATH OF HIS WIFE IN 1884, DOUGLASS MARRIED HELEN PITTS. HE DIED IN WASHINGTON, D.C., ON FEBRUARY 20, 1895.*

Fountain, south side:

> *GABRIEL KOREN, SCULPTOR. ALGERNON MILLER, SITE ARTIST. DECEMBER 2005.*

Frederick Douglass, circa 1879. *National Archives.*

"The flight was a bold and perilous one; but here I am, in the great city of New York, safe and sound, without the loss of blood or bone." This passage etched in granite in the Frederick Douglass memorial comes from his second autobiography, *My Bondage and My Freedom*, and it describes the moment in 1838 when, as a twenty-year-old escaped slave from Maryland, he first set foot in the city. Douglass goes on to explain both the elation and fear that accompanied his arrival in the great metropolis: "In less than a week after leaving Baltimore, I was walking amid the hurrying throng, and gazing upon the dazzling wonders of Broadway. The dreams of my childhood and the promise of my manhood were now fulfilled." And yet Douglass still had reason to fear recapture and could trust no one, not even other African Americans. As he wrote,

> *A sense of my loneliness and helplessness crept over me, and covered me with something bordering on despair. In the midst of thousands of my fellow-men, and yet a perfect stranger! In the midst of human brothers and yet more fearful of them than of hungry wolves.*

While the circumstances of his arrival were unique, Douglass's recounting of the range of emotions inspired by the daunting city is immediately recognizable to anyone who remembers arriving there for the first time and is deserving of its own place of honor in the New York canon.

Given Douglass's undisputed status as one of the greatest abolitionists, writers and orators of the nineteenth century and his special connection to New York, it's to the city's eternal shame that it took until September 20, 2011, 116 years after his death, to honor him with a statue. Nevertheless, the project of building this memorial began, at long last, in 1992, during the administration of the city's first Black Mayor, David Dinkins. It would take nearly two decades to complete. During this time, Harlem added memorials to Duke Ellington (1997), Ralph Ellison (2003), Adam Clayton Powell Jr. (2005) and Harriet Tubman (2008), a sign of the growing influence of Black politicians and the Black community in the city.

In *Sculpture in Gotham: Art and Urban Renewal in New York City*, art historian Michele Bogart, whose book is essential to understanding the forces behind public sculpture in the city, writes in depth about the lengthy community-oriented process behind the Douglass memorial. According to Bogart, much of the impetus for the project came from residents of Towers on the Park and neighboring buildings, who began lobbying the Central Park Conservancy for improvements to Frederick Douglass Circle at 110th and Central Park North.[213] The intersection, named after Douglass in 1950, was made up of four derelict, pie-shaped traffic islands in dire need of a glow up.[214]

In 1995, the Central Park Conservancy held a series of public information sessions and workshops called Help Design! Frederick Douglass Circle. One of the community members involved in the sessions from the beginning was the Black architectural consultant and Harlem historian John Reddick. The "design concept" that emerged from what Reddick described as a "community visioning process" called for, among other things, turning the intersection into a traffic circle like Columbus Circle, a figurative statue of Douglass, a timeline of key events in his life, famous Douglass quotes—and water, because Douglass first came to New York on the water. Also driving the concept was the sense that the Douglass memorial at the northwest corner of the park along with the Ellington memorial at the northeast corner and the recent renovation of the Harlem Meer in the park would make a fitting "Gateway to Harlem."[215] With the guidance and support of Congressman Charles Rangel, the conservancy's project to improve Frederick Douglass Circle secured $15 million in funding from the city, state and U.S. Department of Transportation. $750,000 was set aside for the memorial plaza and statue through the Percent for Art Program.[216]

The job of mounting a public competition to select an artist for the memorial was handed to the Cityscape Institute, which brought John Reddick in to coordinate the process. Reddick had the benefit of having run a similar community-guided process on the memorial to Ralph Ellison. From five finalists, a panel made up of professionals, politicians and Harlem residents, including Reddick, chose the pairing of Algernon Miller and Gabriel Koren. Miller, the main designer, was an African American native of Harlem. Both were known for work they'd done in the city, Miller for an abstract sculpture, *Tree of Hope*, which graced Harlem from 1972 to 2004, and the white, Hungarian-born Koren for her statue of Malcolm X at the Shabazz Center in the old Audubon Ballroom in 1997.[217] In keeping with the community design concept, Miller's winning plan called for a large traffic circle and plaza with a bronze constellation wall depicting the Big

Dipper and the North Star and water underneath. Also included was a bronze figurative statue of Douglass by Koren along with key moments in Douglass's life and passages he wrote etched in the pavement and on granite blocks throughout the space.

Even after winning the contest, Miller and Koren had to go through more layers of public review. Koren, for example, who had modeled her sculpture after photos of Douglass, initially envisioned him as seated, human in scale and accessible to children. However, some called for Douglass to be standing, possibly even on a column like Columbus at the bottom of Central Park West. They were also mindful of another statue down the block, in front of the Museum of Natural History (which was removed in 2022), that of the mounted Teddy Roosevelt flanked by a Native American and an African man, both on foot, in decidedly subservient positions.[218] To compete with the former and compensate for the latter, there was a push for Douglass to be a more monumental presence. Koren pushed back. Having grown up in a communist country, she had an aversion to Soviet-era colossal sculpture. "I don't want empire, I don't want empire," Miller recalled her saying. And so the result was a compromise: a standing Douglass, resplendent in a greatcoat, every inch a man in full and, at eight feet tall, slightly larger than life. He is also facing uptown because, despite the fact that Koren wanted him facing south to maximize the light on his face, the community design concept wanted him facing uptown, symbolically north, toward freedom.

Another snag for Gabriel Koren was her race. In a Cooper Hewitt talk about the Douglass memorial, Reddick described a meeting between Koren, a white lady from Hungary in a headscarf and typical African clothes and "the most African American, African American community board" in the city, Harlem's Community Board 10. Needless to say, the board was skeptical of Koren. But as she began a presentation on her work and it became clear that her subjects were exclusively great Black men, the board members were convinced that she could do the job because they could see that she was, as Reddick put it, "into Black people" and cared deeply about Black history.[219]

While Koren faced headwinds because of her race, Miller got pushback for his representation of Black history. Inspired by claims in the popular history *Hidden in Plain View* that the Underground Railroad used coded quilts to help slaves to freedom, Miller included quilt images in the paving patterns of the plaza, along with two plaques explaining their names and purpose. In 2003, when Miller and Koren presented their plans for the Douglass

Rendering of Frederick Douglass Circle design with original quilt patterns in the pavement. *New York City Public Design Commission Archives.*

memorial to the Art Commission of New York for approval, questions were raised about the historical accuracy of the "freedom quilt" claims, and it was suggested that Miller and Koren verify them with a prominent white historian, Columbia's Eric Foner. Both Miller and Reddick were offended by the suggestion, believed that the white commission members were being patronizing and stood by the design.[220]

Things changed, however, in 2007, when the *New York Times* published an article in which the white Yale historian David Blight slammed the quilt code as "a myth bordering on a hoax." Blight, a Douglass scholar, whose subsequent 2018 biography of the Black leader was highly regarded, pulled no punches, adding, "To permanently associate Douglass's life with this story instead of great, real stories is unfortunate at best." In the same piece, Kate D. Levin, New York's commissioner of cultural affairs, allowed that perhaps different quilt patterns should be used in the memorial for the sake of historical accuracy but opposed getting rid of the quilt images altogether. "Something can inspire an artist that is not…based in fact, " said Levin. "This isn't a work of history, it's a work of art."[221] Ultimately, Miller agreed to change the quilt patterns and remove the plaques about codes in the finished memorial.

The quilt controversy surrounding the Frederick Douglass Memorial raises interesting questions about the line between fact and folklore, as well as history and art. And while quilts may not have contained coded signals, Miller learned that there was a real connection between abolitionists and quilts.[222] With guidance from Chris Moore, a historian from the Schomburg Center for Black Culture, Miller discovered that groups like Boston's Female Anti-Slavery Society organized antislavery fairs at which they sold donated clothing, needlework and quilts for the cause.[223] At a Boston fair in 1836, one such "cradle quilt," likely made by the abolitionist Lydia Child for an infant, had a patchwork of stars, and inscribed in ink on the center panel was a poem with a point:

> *Mother! when around your child*
> *You clasp your arms in love,*
> *And when with grateful joy you raise*
> *Your eyes to God above,*
> *Think of the negro mother, when*
> *Her child is torn away,*
> *Sold for a little slave—oh then*
> *For that poor mother pray!*[224]

Given that quilt makers like Child supported Douglass's tireless fight against slavery, Miller felt that, after the controversy around the quilt patterns, he now had a historical and aesthetic rationale for including them as a foundational element in the Douglass memorial.

Ironically, like Miller, the artist Alison Saar was also inspired by the idea of secret coded quilt blocks and included them in the base of her 2008 Harriet Tubman Memorial, a year after the *Times* ran its story debunking the quilt code myth. For reasons that remain unclear, Saar, unlike Miller, experienced no pushback about her quilt blocks from the city or the public and no criticism in the press.

Chapter 29

ALTHEA GIBSON MONUMENT

Althea Gibson Monument, Eric Goulder, 2019.
David Jacobs.

SCULPTOR: Eric Goulder (1964–)
DEDICATED: August 26, 2019
LOCATION: Billie Jean King National Tennis Center, Flushing Meadows-Corona Park, Queens
ARCHITECT: N/A
MEDIUM: Bronze and granite
DONOR: USTA

Inscription:

> *I hope that I have accomplished just one thing: that I have been a credit to tennis and my country.*

In August 1950, during the most important tennis match of her young career, the twenty-three-year-old Althea Gibson was leading in the third set 7–6, on the verge of a massive upset over Wimbledon champion Louise Brough. Fans were calling out to Brough, "Beat the nigger, beat the nigger" when a thunderstorm abruptly suspended play. On the following day, when the match resumed, Gibson lost—but she would be back.[225]

The tournament was the national women's tennis championship at the West Side Tennis Club in Forest Hills, Queens, the forerunner of today's U.S. Open. Gibson was the first African American ever to receive an invitation. Her presence in the exclusive, lily-white club—where players were also required to wear all white—was made possible in part by an editorial in the July 1950 issue of *American Lawn Tennis* by eighteen-time Grand Slam title winner Alice Marble. In it, Marble criticized Forest Hills for denying Gibson entry: "If Althea Gibson represents a challenge to the present crop of women players, it's only fair that they should meet that challenge," she wrote. "The entrance of Negroes into national tennis is as inevitable as it has proven to be in baseball, in football, or in boxing."[226] Marble's words proved to be prophetic, but she could never have imagined the heights that Gibson would eventually reach.

Althea Gibson was born in 1927 to sharecroppers on a cotton farm in Silver, South Carolina. A few years later, like so many Black families during the Depression, her parents moved to Harlem hoping to escape discrimination and find work. As luck would have it, the Gibsons' apartment on 143rd Street was next to a paddleball court that the Police Athletic League sometimes set up in the street. Tall and athletic, Gibson took to the sport, winning the girls' city championship at age twelve in 1939. Soon after, Harlem's Cosmopolitan Tennis Club, whose members were mostly Black professionals, offered her a membership. In her autobiography, *I Always Wanted to Be Somebody*, Gibson recalled her doubts about the game. "I really wasn't the tennis type," she wrote. "I kept wanting to fight the other player every time I started to lose a match."[227]

Gibson's father, a garage attendant, had doubts about tennis, too. Instead, he taught his aggressive daughter how to box. A poor student, she dropped out of school when she was just thirteen, and when she wasn't playing tennis,

Althea Gibson publicity photo, 1950s. *Wikimedia Commons.*

she roamed the streets getting into fights and hanging out in pool halls. When she came home late, her father beat her—often enough that she went to live in foster care for a time.[228] Gibson had the kind of spirit that made an impression on people even as a teenager. When she saw the boxer Sugar Ray Robinson at a bowling alley, she went right up to him and said, "You're Sugar Ray, aren't you? Well, I can beat you."[229] Charmed by this bold greeting, Robinson became a loyal friend and mentor. He even bought her a saxophone to encourage her love of music.

Fortunately for Gibson, she also found a mentor at the Cosmopolitan Club: Fred Johnson, a one-armed pro. Under his patient tutelage, she channeled her pugnacious instincts and learned the game quickly. In 1942, at age fifteen, she won the New York State Championship, sponsored by the American Tennis Association (ATA), an organization founded by African Americans in 1916 as an alternative to the segregated United States Lawn Tennis Association (USLTA).[230]

In 1946, after losing in the finals of her first ATA women's championship, Gibson was approached by ATA officials Dr. Hubert Eaton and Dr. Robert Johnson, who were looking to develop talented Black players to compete at the highest levels of tennis. "How'd you like to play at Forest Hills some day?" asked Johnson. "Don't kid me," replied Gibson. But Johnson, who would later sponsor and mentor Arthur Ashe, was serious.

Gibson went to live with Dr. Eaton and his wife in Wilmington, North Carolina, which was an adjustment for a young woman who spent her early years brawling in the streets of Harlem. According to *TIME* magazine, her table manners, for example, were so bad that the Eatons initially made her eat in the kitchen. Despite some rough edges, Gibson, at age nineteen, returned to high school, where she took her studies seriously, finishing in three years. In 1949, she received a scholarship from Florida A&M, where she played tennis and basketball.[231]

While she may have been temporarily barred from the Eatons' dining room, she had complete access to their tennis court, where she continued to improve. In the summers, she traveled the ATA circuit with Dr. Johnson, and in 1947, she won her first of ten consecutive ATA women's championships. In 1949, she became the first Black woman to play in a USLTA event, the Eastern Indoor Championships, and got to the semifinals. This tournament, which was the first time Gibson faced white players, impressed the champion Alice Marble so much that she called for Gibson's admission to the 1950 National Championship at Forest Hills.[232] Even though she lost there to Louise Brough, Gibson now had her foot in the door.

In 1951, Gibson played at Wimbledon for the first time, and at five foot eleven, she established herself as an intimidating presence on the women's tour with a big serve and volley game. In 1957, she became the first Black person to win Wimbledon and accepted her trophy from Queen Elizabeth. In her autobiography, she wrote, "Shaking hands with the Queen of England was a long way from being forced to sit in the colored section of the bus." And yet Gibson was still treated like an outcast on the tour. In a 2019 *New York Times* interview, her friend and doubles partner Angela Buxton, from England, recalled, "When I came on the scene the other players wouldn't speak to Althea, much less play with her, quite simply because she was black." Buxton, who was Jewish, felt similarly isolated.[233]

Althea Gibson shakes hands with Queen Elizabeth after winning Wimbledon in 1957. *Wikimedia Commons.*

Gibson's victory at Wimbledon made her a national hero. New York City held a ticker tape parade for her, and an estimated one hundred thousand people lined lower Broadway to catch a glimpse of the first Black woman so honored as she was driven in a convertible to city hall.[234] Gibson appeared on the *Ed Sullivan Show* and on the covers of both *TIME* and *Sports Illustrated*. And she wasn't done yet. Seven years after losing to Louise Brough at Forest Hills, Gibson beat her 6–3, 6–2 in the final to become the first Black woman to win the national championships. Gibson was sometimes called the Jackie Robinson of tennis, but she resisted the comparison, telling a reporter in 1957, "I don't consider myself to be a representative of my people. I'm thinking of me and nobody else."[235] Contrary to Robinson's approach, this attitude, and her refusal to enter the fray of the Civil Rights Movement, lost her the support of many Black people.[236]

In 1958, Gibson defended her titles at Wimbledon and Forest Hills, and she was the no. 1 player in the world. Nonetheless, Gibson chose to retire because at that time, major tournaments were open to amateurs only, so she couldn't make a living playing tennis. After leaving the game, she recorded an album of jazz standards, sang (well) on the *Ed Sullivan Show* and appeared in a John Wayne movie, but she never gained much momentum in either music or film. She picked up golf and, in 1963, became the first Black player on the Ladies Professional Golf Association tour, but she never won a tournament. In the years that followed, Gibson struggled financially and with health issues. While she hadn't taken a stand on civil rights, she did support the next generation of Black players, like Arthur Ashe, who became the first Black man to win Wimbledon in 1975 and credited Gibson with paving the way for him.[237]

In 1990, when Zina Garrison became the first Black woman since Gibson to reach a Wimbledon final, Gibson was there to cheer for her when she lost to Martina Navratilova.[238] Before she died in 2003 at age seventy-six, she had the satisfaction of knowing that the torch had been passed when Venus Williams won the U.S. Open in 1999 and Wimbledon in 2000. Speaking at Gibson's funeral, Garrison recalled spending time with her at Wimbledon: "She showed me the stall where she dressed and where she popped the champagne when she won. She knew she opened the door for all of us, and she was so excited about all the women who followed her."[239] One has to imagine Gibson would be thrilled to see her legacy secured by the unrivaled success of Serena Williams and the emergence of young Black stars Naomi Osaka and Coco Gauff.

In 2019, at the start of the U.S. Open, the United States Tennis Association (USTA) dedicated a monument to Gibson at the Billie Jean King Tennis Center in the shadow of Arthur Ashe Stadium. King, who as a young player was inspired by Gibson, had been lobbying the USTA to honor her for years without luck until some sixth and seventh grade girls from Wilmington, North Carolina, where Althea spent her high school years, got a bee in their collective bonnet. When the girls, members of One Love Tennis, a program for underserved youth, watched the 2014 documentary *Althea* by Rex Miller, they were upset to learn that there was no permanent monument to her—so upset, in fact, that when USTA president Katrina Adams came to visit the program, they handed her a stack of angry letters.[240] "One of them wrote," said Adams in an interview with the *New York Times*, "'Can't you even have a hot-dog stand in her name?' And I'm thinking, *Yeah, I think we can do a little better than a hot-dog stand.*"

As the first Black president of the USTA and a former professional player from the West Side of Chicago, Adams was keenly aware of Gibson's impact on her own career and the game. "If there was no Althea, there'd be no me," she said, "because tennis would not have been so open to me."[241] With the letters from the girls and the support of both Adams and King behind the project, the USTA board unanimously approved the erection of the statue, intentionally within sight of the Arthur Ashe sculpture (see pages 129–132). A diverse group of five artists was asked to submit proposals, and the USTA chose a white sculptor, Eric Goulder.

Goulder trained at the New York Academy of Art, and his conceptual design for the monument features a larger-than-life bronze bust of a youthful Gibson emerging from a granite cube perched on one corner, surrounded by other boxes. The boxes symbolize the way society tried to put Gibson in a box, but as Goulder said in an interview on the podcast *Thirty Love: Conversations About Tennis*, "She [Gibson] turned the box up on edge or on a corner—so that once we see it that way we never see it the other way."[242] Goulder's work is now a regular selfie stop for U.S. Open fans, including Adams.[243] Gibson's shoulder is exposed because, as Goulder explained to the *Washington Post*, "That's the shoulder that everybody since has stood on."[244]

Chapter 30

WOMEN'S RIGHTS PIONEERS MONUMENT

Women's Rights Pioneers Monument, Meredith Bergman. *David Jacobs.*

SCULPTOR: Meredith Bergman
DEDICATED: August 26, 2020
LOCATION: Literary Walk, Central Park
MEDIUM: Bronze; Barre gray granite
SIZE: Group H × W × D: 9'4" × 11'4" × 6'10"
Pedestal H × W × D: 4'8" × 11'8" × 7'2"
DONOR: Monumental Women

Inscription:

Front:

> *SOJOURNER TRUTH, SUSAN B. ANTHONY, ELIZABETH CADY STANTON: WOMEN'S RIGHTS PIONEERS.*

Back:

> *DONATED BY MONUMENTAL WOMEN TO THE CITY OF NEW YORK TO HONOR WOMEN'S HISTORY. DEDICATED ON AUGUST 26, 2020, THE 100TH ANNIVERSARY OF THE RATIFICATION OF THE 19TH "VOTES FOR WOMEN" AMENDMENT TO THE UNITED STATES CONSTITUTION.*

On August 26, 2020, one century after the ratification of the Nineteenth Amendment, which gave women the right to vote, the Women's Rights Pioneers Monument was dedicated in Central Park. Former Secretary of State Hillary Clinton spoke to a small, masked crowd of spectators and local reporters, who had gathered despite the COVID-19 pandemic: "It seems especially appropriate that today on Women's Equality Day we are unveiling a new statue in Central Park for the first time in over six decades. The first statue of real, non-fictional women…the first statue of an African American…and significantly, a statue that depicts three great Americans working together."[245] Those women would be Elizabeth Cady Stanton, Susan B. Anthony and Sojourner Truth, three giants of the abolition and women's suffrage movements.

The movement for the statue was driven by Monumental Women, a nonprofit, all-volunteer organization initially formed in 2014 with the goal of "breaking the bronze ceiling and creating the first statue of real women in Central Park's 167-year history."[246] To make their statue dreams a reality, Monumental Women raised over $1.5 million in private funds, ranging from donors as big as the New York Life Insurance Company to Girl Scout Troops 3483, 3482 and 3746 in New York City.[247] The park has always had statues of women, but they were either allegorical representations, like the angel in Bethesda Fountain, or literary characters like Shakespeare's Juliet or Lewis Carroll's Alice.

Despite Monumental Women's good intentions, when the statue fund released its first design concept in the summer of 2018, it was denounced in the *New York Times* as racist.[248] Like the history of the women's movement, the history of this monument also came with racial controversy.

The concept by the New York artist Meredith Bergman, which was chosen out of ninety-one submissions, featured realistic statues of Stanton seated, Anthony standing and no Sojourner Truth. At that time, Monumental Women was known as the Elizabeth Cady Stanton and Susan B. Anthony Statue Fund, Inc. The fund's intention was to make a statue of the legendary women's rights duo with no other figures in the scene.[249] According to Bergman's artist's statement, the original design allowed for the contributions of other women in the suffrage movement in the form of twenty-two "thought-provoking" quotes on a scroll flowing from Stanton's writing pad to the ground.[250] While there were quotes from African American women like Sojourner Truth, Ida B. Wells and Mary Church Terrell, this form of representation didn't seem to be enough. As Gloria Steinem told the *Times*, "I do think we cannot have a statue of two white women representing the vote for all women."[251]

The Public Design Commission agreed. In March 2019, it called for changes to the design, which included "meaningful ways to acknowledge and commemorate women of color who played an active role in the Woman Suffrage Movement."[252] To appease the critics and the commission, the fund and Bergman revisited her concept and chose to include Sojourner Truth. At the urging of the commission, Bergman consulted on the design with two Black Sojourner Truth historians, Nell Irvin Painter and Margaret Washington, and a white art historian, Darcy Grimaldo. In the summer of 2019, Monumental Women announced the addition of Sojourner Truth to the monument, which the Public Design Commission approved. But this concept also caused controversy, because of Truth's complicated history with Stanton and Anthony.

Sojourner Truth carte de visite, 1864: "I sell the shadow to support the substance." *Library of Congress.*

Sojourner Truth was born into slavery in 1797 as Isabella Baumfree. She grew up on an estate in rural New York and experienced the horrors of slavery: she was beaten, sold, repeatedly raped by her owner and forced to marry and have five children with another slave. After years of torment, Truth found God and the courage to escape slavery, which she did in 1827, with an infant daughter. She began preaching on the evils of slavery and, in 1843, changed her name to Sojourner Truth. Unable to read or write, she dictated *The Narrative of Sojourner Truth, a Northern Slave*, published by William Lloyd Garrison in 1850. On the strength of this compelling account of her enslavement, Truth became a regular on the abolition circuit, along with Frederick Douglass, where her tall, magnetic presence electrified the mostly white crowds.[253]

At the time Sojourner Truth became a national figure, the abolition and women's rights movements were allied in the struggle for human rights. One of the few public figures to embody Blackness and womanhood, Sojourner Truth also began to make a name for herself speaking out for women. She is perhaps best remembered for what came to be known as her "Ain't I a Woman" speech from the 1851 Women's Rights Convention in Akron, Ohio. In recent years, the speech has become a stirring anthem for the rights of Black women, as well as a script for folksy performances on special occasions by Black actresses like Cicely Tyson, Alfre Woodard and Kerry Washington. Unfortunately, this speech, written in a stereotypical Black southern dialect, is one that Sojourner Truth, whose first language was Dutch, never delivered. This speech is in fact the work of the white reformer Frances Gage, who adapted it in dialect for publication in the *New York Independent* during the Civil War in 1863.[254] Gage's well-intentioned aim was to further the cause of abolition and suffrage by giving Truth a southern dialect to make her a more believable slave for northern readers. Instead, she managed to reinforce Black stereotypes while erasing Truth's Dutch heritage and northern slavery history.[255]

Gage wasn't the only white lady with good intentions gone awry. Susan B. Anthony and Elizabeth Cady Stanton were staunch suffragists and abolitionists who both knew and admired Sojourner Truth. The scene in the final version of the Women's Rights Pioneers Monument shows Truth with Anthony and Stanton in a meeting that sculptor Meredith Bergman imagined might have happened at Stanton's New York house during an 1867 American Equal Rights Association (AERA) meeting. All three attended the meeting, during which Truth was a guest in Stanton's home.[256] However, for many historians, this scene is problematic because of a split that occurred in the women's rights movement between Black and white women shortly after.

In 1868, when the proposed Fifteenth Amendment gave Black men the right to vote but not women, both Stanton and Anthony opposed its ratification in

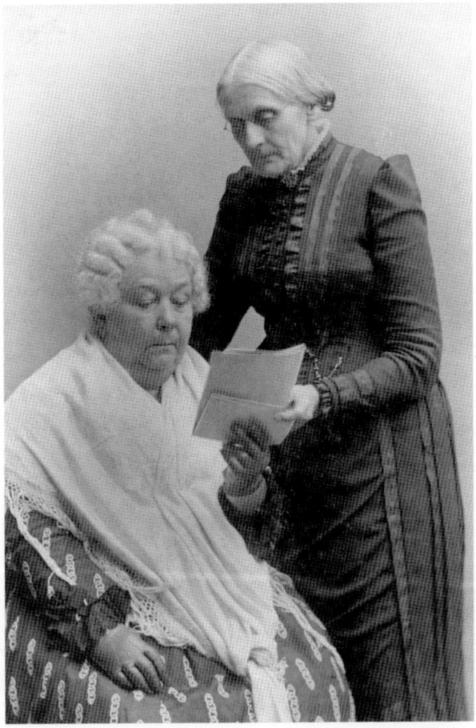

Elizabeth Cady Stanton (*seated*) and Susan B. Anthony, between 1880 and 1902. *Library of Congress.*

no uncertain, often racist, terms. In her suffrage newspaper, *The Revolution*, Stanton infamously wrote, "American women of wealth, education, virtue and refinement, if you do not wish the lower orders of Chinese, Africans, Germans and Irish, with their low ideas of womanhood to make laws for you and your daughters… demand that women too shall be represented in government."[257] Frederick Douglass, an early supporter of women's rights and a friend of both Stanton and Anthony, criticized Stanton's racist screed at an 1869 AERA meeting. He also argued that the vote for Black men was "a matter of life and death" and more urgently needed than the vote for women. At that meeting, Anthony doubled down, responding, "If you will not give the whole loaf of suffrage to the entire people, give it to the most intelligent first. If intelligence, justice, and morality are to have precedence in the government, let the question of women brought up first and that of the negro last."[258]

Stanton and Anthony's racist remarks split the women's rights movement and, some believe, delayed women's suffrage. They also caused an irreparable rift between the Black and women's rights movements, which, one could argue, still remains. Over a century and a half later, their words also made the idea of Sojourner Truth sharing a monument with them unimaginable for some.

Sojourner Truth, for her part, in that same 1869 AERA meeting, offered her unique perspective on the Fifteenth Amendment, saying, "There is a great stir about colored men getting their rights, but not a word about the colored woman; and if colored men get their rights, and not colored women get theirs, there will be a bad time about it."[259] Despite the harsh words, the three seem to have remained on good terms. In 1870, Stanton, responding to a letter from the aging Truth, wrote, "I hope, dear Sojourner, that you will be enfranchised before you leave us for the better land."[260]

Whether you think the Women's Pioneer Monument is appropriate or not, it's worth taking a closer look at the scene. Truth is speaking, and Stanton is poised to write. Anthony is organizing, a traveling bag full of documentation of injustices at her feet. Knitting needles and a ball of yarn lie in Truth's lap. Indeed, many photos of her show her seated with her knitting, because knitting for Union soldiers was seen as the patriotic duty of women during the Civil War. Truth also taught skills like knitting, sewing and cooking to recently freed slaves to help them earn a living.[261]

One last thing to bear in mind about the Women's Rights Pioneer Monument is just how rare it is. Not only is it the first statue of real women in Central Park, but also, out of an estimated 150 public statues of real people in New York City, only seven are of women (the other six being Joan of Arc, Gertrude Stein, Golda Meir, Eleanor Roosevelt, Harriet Tubman and Althea Gibson). Monumental Women is working to correct this imbalance in the city's memorial landscape. As its president, Pam Elam, said at the dedication, "We are all historians trying to rethink the past in order to reshape the future. For what we all seek is nothing less than a full and fair historical record that reflects and respects the contributions of all women and people of color. We won't stop until we win that."[262]

NOTES

Chapter 1

1. "Flowers for the Dead," *Brooklyn Daily Eagle*, May 29, 1876.
2. Andres Schofield, "Black Civil War Soldiers Graves at Green-Wood," Green-Wood Historic Fund, 2020, https://www.green-wood.com.
3. Alan Singer, "Reconstruction Era New York State Democrats: Deserving the 'Execration of History,'" *New York History* 99, no. 2 (2018): 196–208.
4. "The Brilliant Dedication of the Soldiers' Monument," *Springfield Republican*, July 5, 1876.

Chapter 2

5. "Ward Beecher on the Observer: Sharp's Rifles as a Moral Agent," *New York Tribune*, February 8, 1856.
6. Another bronze statue of Beecher featuring an African American woman and girl, by Mount Rushmore's sculptor Gutzon Borglum (1867–1941), is in the Plymouth Church Courtyard. See chapter 6.
7. "Colored Pastors Sympathetic," *Brooklyn Daily Eagle*, March 11, 1887.
8. Edward A. Johnson, *A School History of the Negro Race in America from 1619 to 1890, with a Short Introduction as to the Origin of the Race; Also a Short Sketch of Liberia* (Edwards & Broughton, 1891), 172.
9. "A Half Century, the Concord Baptist Church of Christ Celebrates," *Brooklyn Standard Union*, May 17, 1897.
10. "His Statue Is Unveiled," *New York Times*, June 25, 1891.

Chapter 3

11. "The Dedication Ceremonies," *Brooklyn Daily Eagle*, October 21, 1892.
12. James Hagengruber, "Was This Civil War Hero the First Medal of Honor Recipient Born in Africa?" *Smithsonian Magazine*, June 21, 2023, https://www.smithsonianmag.com.

Chapter 4

13. "World's Greatest Custom House Will Soon Be Completed," *New York Times*, January 1, 1906.
14. "To Adorn New Custom House at Bowling Green," *New York Tribune*, January 17, 1904.
15. Freeman Henry Morris Murray, *Emancipation and the Freed in American Sculpture: A Study in Interpretation* (Legare Street Press), 2022, 92–96.

Chapter 5

16. *Addresses in Memory of Carl Schurz Memorial, Carnegie Hall* (Irving Press, 1906?), 31–48. Available via the Library of Congress, https://www.loc.gov.
17. "Schurz Monument Given to the City," *New York Times*, May 11, 1913.
18. Foner, *Reconstruction Updated Edition*, 500.
19. Sarah Papazoglakis, "A 'Fine Liberal' in Black Radical History: W.E.B. Du Bois's Strategic Citation of Carl Schurz," *American Studies* 58, no. 4 (2019): 97–118.

Chapter 6

20. "Arbuckle Heirs Give $600,000 to Brooklyn," *Brooklyn Daily Eagle*, March 15, 1914.
21. "Plymouth Unveils Statue of Beecher," *Brooklyn Eagle*, October 19, 1914.
22. "The New Beecher Statue," *Standard Union*, October 20, 1914.
23. "Beecher Statue by Sculptor Borglum to Be Erected at Plymouth Church," *Brooklyn Eagle*, September 27, 1912.
24. Lee Boomer, "The Edmonson Sisters: Teaching Black Women's Activism in the 19th Century," New York Historical, February 20, 2018, https://www.nyhistory.org; Samuel Momodu, "The Edmonson Sisters (1832–1895)," BlackPast, September 28, 2016, https://www.blackpast.org.
25. National Register of Historic Places, Registration Form, "Bruin's Slave Jail," https://www.dhr.virginia.gov/VLR_to_transfer/PDFNoms/100-0047_Bruins_Slave_Jail_2000_Final_Nomination.pdf.
26. Debby Applegate, *The Most Famous Man in America: The Biography of Henry Ward Beecher* (Doubleday Books, 2006), 227.
27. National Register of Historic Places, Registration Form, "Bruin's Slave Jail."

Chapter 7

28. Marie Joseph Paul Yves Roch Gilbert du Motier Lafayette, *Memoirs, Correspondence and Manuscripts of General Lafayette* (Saunders and Otley, 1837).
29. George Washington's Mount Vernon, "Lafayette's Testimonial to James Lafayette," https://www.mountvernon.org.
30. John Salmon, "'A Mission of the Most Secret and Important Kind': James Lafayette and American Espionage in 1781," *Virginia Cavalcade* 31 (1981): 78–85.
31. William Waller Hening, ed., *The Statutes at Large, Being a Collection of the Laws of Virginia* (Samuel Pleasants, 1823), 381.
32. Suzanne Spellen and Montrose Morris, "The Man Who Gave Us the Lafayette Statue in Prospect Park," Brownstoner, June 15, 2015, https://www.brownstoner.com.
33. Laura Auricchio, "Lafayette at Yorktown (1782): Transformations and Interpretations," in *A True Friend of the Cause: Lafayette and the Antislavery Movement* (Grolier Club, 2016), 17–31.
34. W.E.B. Du Bois and David Levering Lewis, *Black Reconstruction in America* (Free Press, 1998), 723.

Chapter 8

35. "At Rockefeller Center," *New York Times*, December 24, 1933.
36. Landmarks Preservation Commission, the City of New York, "Rockefeller Center," 1985, https://web.archive.org/web/20171107113311/http://www.neighborhoodpreservationcenter.org/db/bb_files/1985RockefellerCenter.pdf.
37. Daniel Fernandez, "The Pro-Nazi Artist Behind the Brooklyn Public Library's Façade," Hyperallergic, May 24, 2023, https://hyperallergic.com.
38. "*Ein Americaner Nach Hitlers Geschmack* [An American After Hitler's Taste]," *Der Spiegel*, September 10, 2021.

Chapter 9

39. Mary Mullen Cunningham, *Heinze Warneke (1895–1983), A Sculptor First and Last* (University of Delaware Press, 1995), 81–84.
40. "Samuel Memorial Sculptors, Heinz Warneke Correspondence 1936–38," September 22, 1936, Box 127, Folder 1, Archives of the Fairmount Park Association, Historical Society of Pennsylvania, Philadelphia, Pennsylvania.
41. Andy A. Beveridge, "Harlem's Shifting Population." Gotham Gazette, https://www.gothamgazette.com.
42. "River Houses Get Tenants," *New Amsterdam News*, September 4, 1937.
43. "John L. Wilson Jr., 91, Architect of Harlem River Houses, Is Dead," *New York Times*, November 4, 1989.
44. Olin Dows, "Art for Housing Tenants," *Magazine of Art*, November 1938.

45. Dows, "Art for Housing Tenants."
46. "River Houses Sculpture," *New Amsterdam News*, April 9, 1938.

Chapter 10

47. "Sculptor by Accident Is Richmond Barthé," *New Amsterdam News*, October 5, 1938.
48. Margaret Rose Vendryes, *Barthé: A Life in Sculpture* (University Press of Mississippi, 2008), 37–38.
49. Alain Locke, "The Negro in Art," *Christian Education* 15, no. 2 (1931): 101.
50. "Barthé's First One Man Show," *New York Times*, December 18, 1931.
51. Vendryes, *Barthé*, 77–78.
52. Ibid., 87.
53. Jessica Parks, "'Crumbling' Harlem Renaissance Era Frieze at Kingsborough Houses to be Restored," *Brooklyn Paper*, February 11, 2021; Robin Pogrebin, "With Final Gracie Mansion Show, First Lady Aims to Secure Arts Legacy," *New York Times*, February 20, 2020.

Chapter 11

54. Cecile Beaux, "The Spirit of War Memorials," *American Magazine of Art*, May 1919, 270–72.
55. World War I Centennial, "African-Americans," https://www.worldwar1centennial.org.
56. World War I Centennial, "World War 1 Centennial: Honoring Sacrifice, Remembering History," https://worldwar-1centennial.org/.
57. "A Time to Be Honest," *New York Tribune*, February 14, 1919.
58. Ibid.
59. Jeffrey T. Sammons and John H. Morrow Jr., *Harlem's Rattlers and the Great War: The Undaunted 369th Regiment and the African American Quest for Equality* (University Press of Kansas, 2014), 2.
60. Erick Trickey, "One Hundred Years Ago, the Harlem Hellfighters Bravely Led the U.S. into WWI," *Smithsonian Magazine*, May 14, 2018, https://www.smithsonianmag.com.
61. Emmett J. Scott, *Scott's Official History of the American Negro in the World War* (Homewood Press, 1919), 197.
62. Matthew Margis, "A Brief Look at African American Soldiers in the Great War," *Unwritten Record* (blog), February 13, 2017, National Archives and Records Administration, https://unwritten-record.blogs.archives.gov.
63. Sammons and Morrow, *Harlem's Rattlers*, 416.
64. Nora McGreevy, "Quaker Oats to Retire Aunt Jemima After Acknowledging Brand's Origins as 'Racial Stereotype,'" *Smithsonian Magazine*, June 18, 2020, https://www.smithsonianmag.com.

65. "Mrs. Esther Archer, Civic Worker, Points Out Site for Monument," *New York Age*, April 28, 1928.
66. "Another Friend Passes," *New York Age*, October 21, 1944.
67. Eleanor Roosevelt, "My Day, October 2, 1945," Eleanor Roosevelt Papers Digital Edition, 2017, https://erpapers.columbian.gwu.edu/my-day.

Chapter 12

68. "Booker Washington Is Honored Here as Bust Is Added to Hall of Fame," *New York Herald*, May 24, 1946.
69. Booker T. Gardner, "The Educational Contributions of Booker T. Washington," *Journal of Negro Education* 44, no. 4 (1975): 502–18.
70. Library of Congress, "The Civil Rights Act of 1964: A Long Struggle for Freedom," Booker T. Washington's "Atlanta Compromise" Speech, https://www.loc.gov.
71. "Flames Fleeting Nature Is On Display at This Hall," *New York Times*, April 3, 1993.
72. Bronx Community College. "Hall of Fame for Great Americans," March 1, 2022, https://www.bcc.cuny.edu.
73. Chancellor Henry Mitchell MacKracken, "The Hall of Fame," *American Monthly Review of Reviews* 22 (1900): 563, https://onlinebooks.library.upenn.edu/webbin/serial?id=amrevrevs.
74. McCandlish Phillips, "A Spirited Georgian Is Working Resolutely for Her Great American," *New York Times*, September 4, 1965.
75. *The People's Almanac No. 2* (William Morrow & Company, 1978).
76. Mitch Kachun, "'A Beacon to Oppressed Peoples Everywhere': Major Richard R. Wright Sr., National Freedom Day, and the Rhetoric of Freedom in the 1940s," *Pennsylvania Magazine of History and Biography* 128, no. 3 (2004): 279–306.

Chapter 13

77. "A boy gets a closer look" photo, La Guardia & Wagner Archives, https://www.laguardiawagnerarchive.lagcc.cuny.edu.
78. "Statue Dedicated at Lincoln Houses," *New York Times*, February 13, 1949.
79. Box 1, Folder 1, Biographical Statements, Charles Keck Papers, Circa 1905–Circa 1954, Smithsonian Archives of American Art, https://www.aaa.si.edu/collections/charles-keck-papers-9130/series-1/box-1-folder-1.

Chapter 14

80. "Greenland at War," *Life*, September 9, 1943.
81. "Statue in Honor of Coast Guard Planned Here," *New York Herald Tribune*, December 9, 1945; "7 Brave Gun Crews Inspired Memorial," *Pittsburgh Courier*, March 1, 1947.

82. Lieutenant Commander R.F. Barber, "US Coast Guard World War II Memorial," *U.S. Coast Guard Academy Alumni Association Bulletin* 12, no. 1 (April 1950).
83. "7 Brave Gun Crews Inspired Memorial," *Pittsburgh Courier*, March 1, 1947.
84. "Voiceless in Congress," *Pittsburgh Courier*, January 10, 1942.
85. National World War II Museum, "African Americans in World War II: Fighting for a Double Victory," July 2017, https://www.nationalww2museum.org.
86. "7 Brave Gun Crews Inspired Memorial."
87. "Memorial Honors Coastguardsmen," *New York Times*, May 31, 1955.
88. Ibid.; "Her Son Was Killed," *Daily News*, May 31, 1955.
89. John Ott, "Battle Station MoMA: Jacob Lawrence and the Desegregation of the Armed Forces and the Art World," *American Art* 29, no. 3 (2015): 58–89.
90. Author's notes, Admiral K.L. Schultz, prepared remarks, Coast Guard WWII Memorial Rededication, October 4, 2021.

Chapter 15

91. "George Washington Carver," History, October 27, 2009, https://www.history.com.
92. George W. Carver to Robert Durr, October 22, 1937, Box 34, GWC Papers (from *Journal of Negro History*).
93. Barbara Maranzani, "George Washington Carver's Powerful Circle of Friends," Biography.com, January 28, 2021, https://www.biography.com.
94. "Robert Amendola, Instructor to Blind and Sculptor, 86," *New York Times*, January 12, 1996.
95. Carroll Center for the Blind, "Robert Amendola," https://carroll.org.
96. "Robert Amendola, Instructor to Blind And a Sculptor, 86," *New York Times*, January 12, 1996.
97. National Park Service, "Young George Washington Carver Statue," https://www.nps.gov.

Chapter 16

98. "Start Fund for Dr. King Statue in New York City," *Jet Magazine*, November 13, 1969.
99. "Service of Dedication: The Commemorative Heroic Bust in Memory of Dr. Martin Luther King, Jr.," April 4, 1970, https://drive.google.com/file/d/10y9Hpg-WhLFbj9-MJ3mwedGrOD64FxWp.
100. "Announcer Is Expressing Himself as Portrait Sculptor," *Newark Star Ledger*, February 4, 1992.
101. "Rahway Gets Behind Effort to Honor Dr. King," *Newark Star Ledger*, July 7, 1991.

Chapter 17

102. "Salute to Tuskegee," *Chicago Defender*, November 17, 1973.
103. Transcript of John Hope Franklin's Speech at dedication of George Washington Carver bust, April 23, 1977, Bronx Community College Hall of Fame for Great Americans Archive.
104. "A Spirited Georgian Is Working Resolutely for Her Great American," *New York Times*, September 4, 1965.
105. "Stone Wall Jackson Sculpture," *New York Times*, April 8, 1957.
106. Vendryes, *Barthé*, 181.
107. Frances Benjamin Johnston, "George Washington Carver, Half-Length Portrait, Facing Right, Tuskegee Institute, Tuskegee, Alabama," 1906, Library of Congress, https://www.loc.gov/item/98503047.
108. Otis Alexander, "Roscoe C. Brown, Jr. (1922–2016)," BlackPast, April 14, 2024, https://www.blackpast.org.
109. "Cuomo Says Confederate Names on Streets Should Go," *New York Times*, August 16, 2017.

Chapter 18

110. "Colonel Young Softball League Seeking Lights," *New Amsterdam News*, November 14, 1981.
111. Martin Luther King, Jr. Research and Education Institute, "Robinson, Jackie," https://kinginstitute.stanford.edu.
112. NYC Parks, "Jackie Robinson," https://www.nycgovparks.org.
113. "Frederick Samuels Dies at 61: 3-Term Harlem Councilman," *New York Times*, September 13, 1985.
114. *Local Laws of the City of New York for the Year 1978*, New York City Municipal Archives, 290, 346.
115. "Inge Hardison, Actress and Sculptor of Heroes, Dies at 102," *New York Times*, April 5, 2016.
116. "Negro Giants in History," Alva Museum Replicas, Inc. brochure, date unknown (after 1968).
117. "A Sculptor of Black Heroes Leaves a Legacy," *New York Times*, May 26, 2016.
118. "Acclaimed Sculptor Inge Hardison Passes at 102," *New Amsterdam News*, April 14, 2016.

Chapter 19

119. "New York City's Robert Pugh," *Stone in America*, April 1981.
120. Zion Baptist Church, "History of Zion Baptist Church," http://www.zbc523.org.
121. Albert Davila, "Boro Rites for King," *New York Daily News*, January 16, 1981; "Their Elders Promise They Won't Forget," *New York Times*, January 16, 1981.
122. A. Leon Lowry II, conversation with author, July 24, 2024.

123. *Local Laws for the City of New York, 1981*, NYC Municipal Reference Library, 735.
124. "Negroes Call of Brooklyn Pickets As Governor Acts," *New York Times*, August 7, 1963.
125. David Halberstam, "Negro Ministers To Aid Crime Fight," *New York Times*, June 12, 1964.
126. Letter from Officers of Zion Baptist Church to Borough President Howard Golden, June 1, 1981, courtesy of NYC Parks Department Lowry Monument File.
127. Diana Chapin, NYC Parks Department Memo on Monument, October 20, 1980.
128. *Local Laws for the City of New York for the Year 1986; No. 50*, NYC Municipal Reference Library.

Chapter 20

129. "Requiem for a Hero," *Ebony*, May 1986.
130. John Brunelli, "Astronaut Ron McNair Delivers the Commencement at the University of South Carolina," August 1984, YouTube, https://youtu.be/hXHgFtP4EjQ.
131. Commemorative Landscapes, "Dr. Robert E. McNair Memorial, Greensboro," https://docsouth.unc.edu.
132. *Local Laws for the City of New York, 1986; No. 50.*
133. Jennifer McGregor, email to author, July 17, 2024.
134. NYC Cultural Affairs Department, "Percent for Art," https://www.nyc.gov/site/dclapercentforart/about.
135. LINKLaV, "Sculptor Ogundipe Fayomi," YouTube, 2008, https://youtu.be/V0B5bww3Pjg.
136. Fayomi Ogundipe, conversation with author, July 16, 2024.
137. New York City Department of Parks & Recreation, "Dr. Ronald McNair Park," https://www.nycgovparks.org.

Chapter 21

138. "Where Imaginations Run Wild," *New York Times*, June 21, 1997.
139. Ezra Jack Keats Foundation, "Ezra's Bio," https://www.ejkf.org.
140. "Ezra Jack Keats, 67, Is Dead," *New York Times*, May 7, 1983.
141. Ezra Jack Keats Foundation, "Ezra's Bio."
142. New York Public Library, "Top Ten Checkouts of All Time," https://www.nypl.org.
143. Tupper Thomas, conversation with author, September 19, 2024.
144. Excerpts of interview with Debra Pope about Peter and Willie, provided by Ezra Jack Keats Foundation.
145. Auction Finds, "The Mystical Talents of Artist Otto Neals," February 1, 2021, https://myauctionfinds.com.
146. Otto Neals, "Home," https://www.ottonealsart.com.

147. "New Otto Neals' Sculpture Mounted at Prospect Park," *New Amsterdam News*, June 1997.
148. Christian Zimmerman, conversation with author, July 2024.

Chapter 22

149. "After an 18 Year Campaign, an Ellington Memorial Rises," *New York Times*, July 1, 1997.
150. Britannica, "Duke Ellington," https://www.britannica.com.
151. PBS, "The Story of 'Take the A Train,' Duke Ellington's Signature Song," https://www.pbs.org.
152. DIVA (San Francisco State University), "Ralph Gleason on Duke Ellington," https://diva.sfsu.edu.
153. "After an 18-Year Campaign."
154. "Ellington Sculpture Puts Some Critics in a Mood Indigo," *New York Times*, May 4, 1990.
155. Bob Herbert, "Unsophisticated Ladies," *New York Daily News*, May 3, 1990.
156. "Returning Duke's Love for a City," *New York Times*, July 2, 1997.
157. "After an 18-Year Campaign."

Chapter 23

158. "Nude Serves Up Mixed Feelings," *New York Newsday*, August 29, 2000; "Statue for Ashe Creates Confusion," *New York Times*, August 29, 2000.
159. "Sports Guy Stands Tall Sans Towel," *New York Times*, September 7, 2000.
160. Ibid.
161. Judy Levering, conversation with author, August 14, 2024.
162. Michael Ainslie, conversation with author, August 14, 2024.
163. "In Capturing Star, Artist Goes for Spirit," *New York Times*, September 1, 2000.
164. "USTA Billie Jean King National Tennis Center Quick Facts," https://s3.amazonaws.com/ustaassets/assets/1/15/2._2016_mg_facility_and_grounds.9.pdf.
165. Jeanne Moutoussamy-Ashe, "A New Year's Gift for Richmond: Accept Gift of Arthur's Vision," *Richmond Times Dispatch*, January 1, 1996.
166. Virginia Museum of History and Culture, "Sketch of Arthur Ashe, by Paul DiPasquale, 1993," https://virginiahistory.org.

Chapter 24

167. Hilton Als, "In the Territory: A Look at the Life of Ralph Ellison," *New Yorker*, April 30, 2007.
168. PBS, "Ralph Ellison's Life and Career Timeline," https://www.pbs.org.
169. "Neighborhood Report: Harlem; Art to Make a Writer Visible for the Ages," *New York Times*, November 18, 2001.
170. John Reddick, conversation with author, August 19, 2024.

171. Lynn Norment, "Elizabeth Catlett: Legendary Artist Is Still Creating and Living Life on Her Own Terms," *Ebony*, March 2006.
172. Samella S. Lewis, *African American Art and Artists* (University of California Press, 2003), 134.
173. "Memorial to Famed Author Ralph Ellison Is Unveiled in New York," *Jet*, May 19, 2003.
174. Elizabeth Catlett, "Art in Public Places," Museum of African American Art Los Angeles, 1987, quoted in *Elizabeth Catlett: A Black Revolutionary Artist and All That It Implies*, edited by Dalila Scruggs (University of Chicago Press, 2024), 244–45.

Chapter 25

175. Thomas A. Johnson, "A Man of Many Roles," *New York Times*, April 5, 1972.
176. Martin Luther King, Jr. Research and Education Institute, "Powell, Adam Clayton, Jr.," https://kinginstitute.stanford.edu.
177. American Archive of Public Broadcasting (GBH and the Library of Congress), "The Great Depression; Interview with Adam Clayton Powell III. Part 1," Film and Media Archive, Washington University in St. Louis, http://americanarchive.org/catalog/cpb-aacip-151-zp3vt1hh34.
178. "The Congress: The Curse of Adam," *Time Magazine*, January 13, 1967; "Huff Wins Miss Ohio," *Oil City Derrick*, July 5, 1960.
179. George Goodman Junior, "Hundreds of Mourners Pay Respects to Powell," *New York Times*, April 9, 1972.
180. "Two Harlem Streets Named for Civil Rights Leaders," *New York Times*, November 9, 2009.
181. "New York Day By Day; Name Change to Honor a Harlem Hero," *New York Times*, July 20, 1983.
182. Branly Cadet, conversation with author, September 10, 2024.
183. Arthur Ashe Legacy at UCLA, "The Mixed Legacy of Adam Clayton Powell, Jr.," February 15, 2016, https://arthurashe.ucla.edu.
184. Andrew Glass, "New York Voters Restore Powell to His Congressional Seat, April 11, 1967," Politico, April 11, 2019, https://www.politico.com.
185. Cadet, conversation with author.
186. "Honoring Mr. Civil Rights with a Statue of His Likeness," *New Amsterdam News*, February 24, 2005.
187. Dr. Will Brown Jr., conversation with author, September 12, 2024.

Chapter 26

188. "What a Big Leaguer Gets in the Mail," *Pittsburgh Courier*, April 26, 1947.
189. "Robinson Reveals Written Threats; Dodgers' Negro Star Told to 'Get Out of Baseball,'" *New York Times*, May 10, 1947.
190. "Bigwigs of Baseball Support Jackie Robinson," *Pittsburgh Courier*, May 17, 1947.
191. "Pee Wee Day Monumental," *New York Daily News*, November 2, 2005.

192. "Pee Wee, Jackie: Together Again?" *Newsday*, December 14, 2003.
193. Archives of the Mayor's Press Office, "Mayor Giuliani Announces Statue of Brooklyn Dodger Greats Jackie Robinson and Pee Wee Reese to be Built in Brooklyn," December 2, 1999, https://www.nyc.gov.
194. Suzanne Randolph, conversation with author, September 13, 2024.
195. Ibid.
196. Ira Berkow, "Two Men Who Did the Right Thing," *New York Times*, November 2, 2005.
197. Brian Cronin, "Did Reese Really Embrace Robinson in '47?" *ESPN Magazine*, April 13, 2013.
198. Carl T. Rowan, with Jackie Robinson, *Wait 'Til Next Year: The Life Story of Jackie Robinson* (Ishi Press, 1960).
199. Berkow, "Two Men."
200. Ibid.

Chapter 27

201. PBS LearningMedia, "Harriet Tubman: Visions of Freedom," https://ny.pbslearningmedia.org.
202. National Park Service, "Harriet Tubman and the Underground Railroad," https://www.nps.gov.
203. Harriet Tubman Biography, "Home," http://harriettubmanbiography.com.
204. American Masters Digital Archive (WNET), "Alison Saar," Unladylike2020: The Changemakers, February 18, 2020, https://www.pbs.org.
205. Catherine Clinton, *Harriet Tubman: The Road to Freedom* (Little, Brown, 2017), 151–61.
206. Frederick Douglass, "1868: Letter from Frederick Douglass to Harriet Tubman," BlackPast, https://www.blackpast.org.
207. Herb Boyd, "Several Plazas Planned for Harlem," *New Amsterdam News*, October 31, 2007.
208. City of New York Parks & Recreation and NYC Department of Cultural Affairs, "*Swing Low*: Harriet Tubman Memorial Sculpture Is Dedicated in Harlem," press release, November 13, 2008, https://www.nyc.gov.
209. "Why Is Harriet Tubman Facing South?" *New York Times*, November 13, 2008.
210. National Park Service, "Myths & Facts About Harriet Tubman," https://www.nps.gov.
211. Ibid.
212. "Swing Low: Harriet Truman Memorial in Harlem," *New Amsterdam News*, March 21, 2012.

Chapter 28

213. Michele H. Bogart, *Sculpture in Gotham: Art and Urban Renewal in New York City* (Reaktion Books, 2018), 201–02.

214. NYC Planning, "ZoLa: New York City's Zoning & Land Use Map," https://zola.planning.nyc.gov.
215. Central Park Conservancy, "Establishing a 'Gateway to Harlem': The Creation of Frederick Douglass Circle," February 4, 2021, https://www.centralparknyc.org.
216. "In Douglass Tribute Slave Folklore and Fact Collide," *New York Times*, January 23, 2007.
217. Bogart, *Sculpture in Gotham*, 207–08.
218. The Roosevelt statue, which was dedicated in 1940, was removed by the museum in 2022, in the wake of the murder of George Floyd, for its discomfiting suggestion of a racial hierarchy.
219. Cooper Hewitt, "Harlem Focus | Public Monuments: Art in Collaboration with Landscape Design," May 8, 2013, https://www.cooperhewitt.org.
220. Bogart, *Sculpture in Gotham*, 211; Jonathan Reddick, conversation with author, August 19, 2024.
221. "In Douglass Tribute, Slave Folklore and Fact Collide," *New York Times*, January 23, 2007.
222. Cooper Hewitt, "Harlem Focus."
223. Kelsey Gustin, "The Anti-slavery Fair," Boston Public Library blog, August 8, 2018, https://www.bpl.org.
224. Historic New England, "Cradle Quilt," https://www.historicnewengland.org.

Chapter 29

225. Sally H. Jacobs, "Althea Gibson, Tennis Star Ahead of Her Time, Gets Her Due at Last," *New York Times*, August 26, 2019.
226. Alice Marble, "A Vital Issue," *American Lawn Tennis: The Illustrated Magazine of the Game* (July 1, 1950).
227. Jacobs, "Althea Gibson."
228. Robert McG. Thomas Jr., "Althea Gibson, First Black Wimbledon Champion, Dies at 76," *New York Times*, September 28, 2003.
229. "That Gibson Girl," *Time Magazine*, August 26, 1957.
230. Thomas Jr., "Althea Gibson."
231. "That Gibson Girl."
232. Richard E. Lapchick, "Althea Gibson Must Be Smiling over Venus, Serena," March 3, 2009, UCF Today, https://www.ucf.edu.
233. Jacobs, "Althea Gibson."
234. Alliance for Downtown New York, "History of New York City's Ticker-Tape Parades," 2019, https://downtownny.com.
235. Jacobs, "Althea Gibson."
236. Ibid.
237. Lapchick, "Althea Gibson."
238. Thomas Jr., "Althea Gibson."

239. Ibid.
240. Ben Steelman, "Wilmington Youths Help Gain Statue for Althea Gibson," *Wilmington StarNews*, March 23, 2018, https://www.starnewsonline.com.
241. Jacobs, "Althea Gibson"; Katrina Adams, interview with author, November 6, 2024.
242. *Thirty Love: Conversations About Tennis* (podcast), "Artist Eric Goulder on His Althea Gibson Sculpture at the US Open," August 27, 2019.
243. Adams, interview with author.
244. "At US Open," *Washington Post*, September 5, 2019.

Chapter 30

245. CBS New York, "New Central Park Monument Pays Tribute to Women's Rights Pioneers," August 26, 2020, https://youtu.be/2L_lw6K4bzI.
246. Monumental Women, "About," March 31, 2024, https://monumentalwomen.org.
247. Pam Elam, "Women's Rights Pioneers Monument Unveiling Speech," August 26, 2020, https://monumentalwomen.org.
248. Ginia Bellafante, "Is a Planned Monument to Women's Rights Racist?" *New York Times*, January 17, 2019.
249. Alisha Haridasani Gupta, "For Three Suffragists, a Monument Well Past Due," *New York Times*, August 6, 2020.
250. Meredith Bergman, "Artist's Statement, Project, Scope and Narrative," NYC Public Design Application, Conceptual Review, September 2018.
251. Bellafante, "Planned Monument."
252. NYC Public Design Commission Certificate, Public Design Commission, March 18, 2018.
253. Nell Irvin Painter, *Sojourner Truth: A Life, a Symbol* (W.W. Norton, 1997).
254. Sojourner Truth Memorial Committee, "Her Words," February 11, 2013, https://sojournertruthmemorial.org.
255. Sojourner Truth Project, https://www.thesojournertruthproject.com.
256. Bergman, "Artist's Statement."
257. Elizabeth Cady Stanton, "The Sixteenth Amendment," *The Revolution*, April 29, 1869.
258. National Park Service, "Why the Women's Rights Movement Split over the 15th Amendment," https://www.nps.gov.
259. Ibid.
260. Sojourner Truth, *Narrative of Sojourner Truth* […] (Review and Herald Office, 1884), 297. Available via Documenting the American South, https://docsouth.unc.edu/neh/truth84/truth84.html.
261. Jennifer Lindsay, "Reflecting on Sojourner Truth in Honor of Black History Month 2021," Center for Knit & Crochet Digital Museum, https://centerforknitandcrochet.org.
262. Pam Elam, "Dedication Remarks," Monumental Women, August 26, 2020, https://monumentalwomen.org.

SELECTED BIBLIOGRAPHY

Applegate, Debby. *The Most Famous Man in America: The Biography of Henry Ward Beecher*. Doubleday Books, 2006.

Auricchio, Laura. *The Marquis: Lafayette Reconsidered*. Presidio Press, 2015.

Bogart, Michele H. *Public Sculpture and the Civic Ideal in New York City, 1890–1930*. Smithsonian Institution Scholarly Press, 1997.

———. *Sculpture in Gotham: Art and Urban Renewal in New York City*. Reaktion Books, 2018.

Caro, Robert A. *The Power Broker: Robert Moses and the Fall of New York*. Vintage Books, 1974.

Caroli, Betty Boyd. *First Ladies: From Martha Washington to Michelle Obama*. Oxford University Press, 2010.

Clinton, Catherine. *Harriet Tubman: The Road to Freedom*. Little, Brown, 2017.

Cunningham, Mary Mullen. *Heinz Warneke, 1895–1983: A Sculptor First and Last*. University of Delaware Press, 1995.

Durante, Dianne L. *Outdoor Monuments of Manhattan: A Historical Guide*. New York University Press, 2007.

Fischl, Eric. *Bad Boy*. Crown Business, 2014.

Foner, Eric. *Reconstruction Updated Edition: America's Unfinished Revolution, 1863–1877*. HarperCollins, 2024.

Gayle, Margot, and Michele Cohen. *The Art Commission and Municipal Art Society Guide to Manhattan's Outdoor Sculpture*. Prentice Hall Press, 1988.

Gilbert, Olive. *Narrative of Sojourner Truth, a Northern Slave: Emancipated from Bodily Servitude by the State of New York, in 1828*. Franklin Classics, 2018.

Gill, Jonathan. *Harlem: The Four Hundred Year History from Dutch Village to Capital of Black America*. Grove Press/Atlantic Monthly Press, 2012.

Holzer, Harold. *Monument Man: The Life and Art of Daniel Chester French*. Princeton Architectural Press, 2019.

Krahe, Diane, and Theodore Catten. "Walking In Credence: An Administrative History of George Washington Carver National Monument." National Park Service, 2014. https://npshistory.com/publications/gwca/adhi.pdf.

Lewis, Samella S. *African American Art and Artists*. University of California Press, 2003.

Murray, Freeman Henry Morris. *Emancipation and the Freed in American Sculpture: A Study in Interpretation*. Legare Street Press, 2022.

Ott, John. "Battle Station MoMA: Jacob Lawrence and the Desegregation of the Armed Forces and the Art World." *American Art* 29, no. 3 (2015): 58–89. doi:10.1086/684920.

The People's Almanac #2. William Morrow, 1978.

Rooney, Sierra, Jennifer Wingate and Harriet F. Senie, eds. *Teachable Monuments: Using Public Art to Spark Dialogue and Confront Controversy*. Bloomsbury Visual Arts, 2021.

Sammons, Jeffrey T., and John H. Morrow Jr. *Harlem's Rattlers and the Great War: The Undaunted 369th Regiment and the African American Quest for Equality*. University Press of Kansas, 2014.

Savage, Kirk. *Standing Soldiers, Kneeling Slaves: Race, War, and Monument in Nineteenth-Century America*. Princeton University Press, 2018.

Snyder, Cal. *Out of Fire and Valor: The War Memorials of New York from the Revolution to 9/11*. Bunker Hill Publishing, 2005.

Taft, Lorado. *The History of American Sculpture*. Franklin Classics, 2018.

Vendryes, Margaret Rose. *Barthé: A Life in Sculpture*. University Press of Mississippi, 2008.

Selected Newspapers

Brooklyn Daily Eagle
Brooklyn Paper
Brooklyn Standard Union
Chicago Defender
Los Angeles Times
Newark Star Ledger
New Amsterdam News
New York Age
New York Daily News
New York Herald
New York Newsday
New York Times
New York Tribune
Oil City Derrick
Pittsburgh Courier
Richmond Times Dispatch
Springfield Republican
Washington Post
Wilmington Star News

Selected Magazines and Journals

American Art News
American Lawn Tennis: The Illustrated Magazine of the Game
American Magazine of Art
Der Spiegel
Ebony
Jet
Journal of Negro Education
Life Magazine
Magazine of Art

The New Yorker
Pennsylvania Magazine of History and Biography
Stone in America
TIME

Selected Interviews and Discussions

Katrina Adams
Michael Ainslie
Michele Bogart
Dr. William Brown Jr.
Branly Cadet
Gordon Davis
Philip J. Dempsey
Ogundipe Fayomi
Kendall Henry
Jonathan Kuhn
Judy Levering
A. Leon Lowry II
Suzanne Randolph
John T. Reddick
Nancy Rosen
Tupper Thomas
Valerie Velazquez de Louzonis
Christian Zimmerman

ABOUT THE AUTHOR

David Felsen teaches eleventh-grade American history at Avenues The World School in New York City. He has an MA in American history from the Gilder Lehrman Institute of American History at Pace University and a BA in history from Haverford College. Before becoming a history teacher, David produced documentaries for HBO, PBS and History, among others. He lives in Brooklyn near Prospect Park with his wife, his son, a dog and a cat.